WO
THROUGH MY LENS

SANDHYA DESHPANDE

INDIA · SINGAPORE · MALAYSIA

Notion Press

No.8, 3rd Cross Street
CIT Colony, Mylapore
Chennai, Tamil Nadu – 600004

First Published by Notion Press 2021
Copyright © Sandhya Deshpande 2021
All Rights Reserved.

ISBN 978-1-63781-575-5

This book has been published with all efforts taken to make the material error-free after the consent of the author. However, the author and the publisher do not assume and hereby disclaim any liability to any party for any loss, damage, or disruption caused by errors or omissions, whether such errors or omissions result from negligence, accident, or any other cause.

While every effort has been made to avoid any mistake or omission, this publication is being sold on the condition and understanding that neither the author nor the publishers or printers would be liable in any manner to any person by reason of any mistake or omission in this publication or for any action taken or omitted to be taken or advice rendered or accepted on the basis of this work. For any defect in printing or binding the publishers will be liable only to replace the defective copy by another copy of this work then available.

Cover Design by Dr. Sadanand Choudhary.

Dedication

Dedicated to my beloved mother,
Late Smt. Urmila Sharma, who always trusted and
boosted my potentials.

Inspiration

Inspired by **Dr. Lokendra Singh**, who ignited my mind to write this book.

Ms Sandhya Deshpande is a very innovative, dedicated, affectionate and a unique science teacher in one of the leading Educational Institute of central India [Nagpur]. I have known her for last one and half year when I met her in a school debate competition where I was the Chairperson and again when I was invited as a chief guest to inaugurate a knowledge centre in a reputed city college at Nagpur. She has vast teaching experience of more than two and half decades. It's really good to know that she considers herself still a learner even at such a senior position. In this book she has written many wonderful incidences, situations and thoughts which came to her mind due to her keen observant nature. She feels that these all episodes and incidences are very close to her heart. When it comes from the pen of such an accomplished and talented teacher, I am sure these don't remain just inspiring stories and true-life experiences but act as great pearls of wisdom so useful for teachers and parents alike. It can be a guiding light even.

The book is written in a very lucid manner and is straight from the heart so the readers can feel the emotions with true intensity. Unfortunately, in this era of rampant commercialisation and life's rat race good parenting and teaching is totally neglected. The emotional connect between teacher and students is totally lacking. This book, I am sure, will help young generation in becoming emotionally strong to handle tough situations of life. There are 55 chapters in all, which are short write ups, stories, essays etc. All are very meaningful, thoughtful and have a lot to offer as take away message. The book is titled as 'World Through My Lens' and it indeed is.

I wish Ms Deshpande all the best for her maiden publication and many more will follow the suit, I am sure.

– Dr. Lokendra Singh
Consultant Neurosugeon,
Director central india institute of medical sciences Nagpur,
President of Neurological society of India,
Maharashtra Hindi Sahitya academy awardee poet,
Writer of many literary books in English

Best Wishes for the Book

Shri Nitin Gadkari

नितीन गडकरी
NITIN GADKARI

मंत्री
सड़क परिवहन एवं राजमार्ग;
सूक्ष्म, लघु एवं मध्यम उद्यम
भारत सरकार
Minister
Road Transport and Highways;
Micro, Small and Medium Enterprises
Government of India

Smt. Sandhya Deshpande,

D. O. NO. 2069
DATE 2 MAR 2021

I am happy to learn that Mrs. Sandhya Deshpande has penned a book named 'A World Through My Lens'. She is a teacher by profession. Tearchers shape the future of generations. Mrs. Sandhya Deshpande has painstakingly tried to balance the relationship amongst students, parents and teachers to achieve better output through the process of teaching and learning.

This book will guide teachers and parents about the basics of parenting thereby creating the responsible and sensible citizens of this great nation.

I extend my best wishes to Mrs. Sandhya Deshpande for this endeavour and hope to see such books being published by devoted teachers like her.

With warm regards.

Yours,

(Nitin Gadkari)

Room No. 501, Transport Bhawan, 1, Sansad Marg, New Delhi – 110 001, Tel.: (RTH) 011-23710121, 23711252 (O), 23719023 (F),
Room No. 51, Ground Floor, Udyog Bhawan, Rafi Marg, New Delhi – 110 011, Tel.: (MSME) 011-23061566, 23061739 (O), 23063141 (F),
Camp Office Nagpur: Plot No. 234, Hill Road, Shivaji Nagar, Between Ramnagar Chowk to Gandhi Nagar Chowk, Nagpur | Tel.: 0712-2239920, 23, 24, 26, 18
E-mail: nitin.gadkari@nic.in; website-www.morth.nic.in / https://msme.gov.in

Shri Daya Shankar Tiwari

नागपूर महानगरपालिका, नागपूर

दयाशंकर च. तिवारी
महापौर

फोन.(का.) : 0712-2567000
फॅक्स (का.): 0712-2567000
महानगरपालिका मार्ग, सिव्हील
लाईन्स, नागपूर – 440001
twitter- t_dayashankar
Instagram - dayatiwari_63
दि : ११.०२.२०२१

प्रमाणपत्र

श्रीमती संध्या देशपांडे ने मुझे नवोदित लेखिका के रूप में कई प्रकार से प्रभावित किया है। वे एक विज्ञान की शिक्षिका हैं । स्वाभाविक है कि उनकी भावना तथा सारे अध्याय वैज्ञानिक यथार्थ से बहुत दूर नहीं रह सकते हैं । खुद का अलग दृष्टिकोण होने के कारण ही उनकी पुस्तक का शीर्षक "World through My Lens " है । ये बहुत हद तक उचित भी है । अपने रोजमर्रा के अनुभवों को अत्यंत ही सरल व प्रभावी ढंग से प्रस्तुत किया है । उनकी सारी रचनाएं बेहद अर्थपूर्ण और शिक्षकों, पालकों तथा विद्यार्थियों व समाज के हर वर्ग को प्रेरित करने की क्षमता रखती हैं ।

अपने अनुभवों को कल्पना की डोर से बाँधकर उन्होंने उसे जनमानस तक पहुँचाने का एक सफल प्रयास किया है । मुझे आशा है कि उनकी इस किताब को अच्छा प्रतिसाद मिलेगा, और सभी का आशीर्वाद प्राप्त होगा मेरी शुभकामनाएँ हैं । और ये आशा है कि वे अपनी रचनाओं से साहित्य भंडार को समृद्ध करेंगी साथ ही साथ समाज उत्थान में भी उनका बहुत योगदान रहेगा ।

शुभकामनाओं के साथ ।

(दयाशंकर तिवारी)

निवास : 1038, डॉ. श्यामाप्रसाद मुखर्जी मार्ग, हंसापुरी, नागपूर
फोन. : 0712-2728257 मो. : 9823293001 व्हॉटसअॅप : 9373107164

Dr. Nilotpala Pradhan

Dr. Nilotpala Pradhan.
Principal Scientist & Associate Professor in AcSIR
(Biological Sciences)
Environment & Sustainability Department,
CSIR-Institute of Minerals & Materials Technology,
Bhubaneswar-751013, Odisha, India.

Dear Sandhya,

When I sat to write about you, I got lost in memories of my adolescent years of our life, when we were growing up together as an adult but still had the innocence of a child. I still remember, when I met you for the first time, on the first day of our new school, when we were in class 8 after the transfer of my father to Nagpur. My father had a transferable job and every few years everything used to change, place, school, everything except family. Most importantly I used to lose my old friends and make new ones. At present, you are such a friend, whom l know for the longest period. A few years back we met again, face to face, after a gap of 16-17 years, but you have not changed much. You are the same enthusiastic, energetic, *chulbuli*, loving, *baat baat har hasne aur hasane wali* my dear 'Rekha'. Also, now you have a great sense of humor and an incredibly long-lasting memory. The qualities which you have, are beautifully harnessed to make you a wonderful writer. I greatly enjoy reading your published and unpublished articles.

I always admire you and feel lucky to have you as my friend. If any time I get any doubts and want to know how much the years and circumstances have changed me, I can ask you. I know you can give your frank opinion about positive and negative changes in me. But I also know that you will only tell me about the positive changes because you have an inherent capacity to see only positive things in people and situations. This quality has remained with you since childhood and you have very well-nourished it. This positive attitude gives you your smiling face and compassionate heart within.

I pray to God to continue giving his blessings to you. May He shower on you, all the happiness in life.

Yours loving

Niloo

(Nilotpala Pradhan)

Disclaimer

This work is inspired by true events, yet all the names, characters, businesses, places, events and incidents in this book are either the product of the author's imagination or used in a fictitious manner. Any resemblance to actual persons, living or dead, or actual events is purely coincidental.

Acknowledgements

- To my father Shri. Jagannath Prasad Sharma, who believed in educating all his daughters well, so that they can be independent mentally and financially.

- To my husband Shri. Sanjay Deshpande, Smt. Malati Deshpande, Shri. Vasantrao Deshpande, Sau. Pushpa Kaku and my sisters—Usha *didi*, Dr. Anjali, Rakhi, Laxmi, and their families, and my brother Suraj, who always encouraged and appreciated me for every small achievement to reach here.

- My loving son Yug and sweet daughter Shiwali, who were the first people to listen and give their valuable feedback for further improvement.

- To the management, my mentor Smt. Annapurni Shastri, Director Bharatiya Vidya Bhavan, Nagpur Kendra and Principal Smt. Anju Bhutani of Bhavan's B.P. Vidya Mandir, Civil Lines, Nagpur, who believed in me and gave me ample opportunities to grow as an individual with complete mental freedom.

- To the Editor of 'The Hitavada', for being kind enough to publish so many articles that ultimately helped me in realising my potential.

- To my senior colleague, Late Smt. Maya Tiwari and a close friend Smt. Sangeeta Batra, who read all my scribblings and appreciated, motivated, and encouraged me like a growing child.

- To my fourth floor staffroom friends who have always given a patient hearing to whatever I wrote and liked it. This too helped my trembling feet get firmness.

- To each and every member of my creative family, '*The Creative Luminaries*', that includes eminent writers like Dr. Lokendra Singh, Dr. Rajesh Iyer, Dr. Sumit Paul, Dr. Sanjay Jain, and so many others.

- To Dr. Sadanand Choudhary, for taking creative pains and efforts to design such a beautiful cover page of my book.

- To Ojas InfoTech for all the technical help needed every now and then.

- To my students, their parents, my friends, well-wishers from the cross-section of society who have taken the risk of converting a Science teacher into a Poet, Writer, Singer, Debater etc.

- Finally, I would like to thank Notion Press for publishing my manuscript. I am thankful to the editor, with whom I struck rapport from the word go, for evaluating, editing and fine tuning of my manuscript.

Contents

Dedication 3
Inspiration 4
Best Wishes for the Book 6
Disclaimer 12
Acknowledgements 13

1. 'I Shouldn't be Alive' 19
2. How I became a Writer 23
3. My First Class 26
4. The Haunting Backstage 29
5. Emotional Connection 32
6. Attention 35
7. Anger and Laughter 38
8. Picnic and Panic 40
9. Out-of-the-Box Techniques 43
10. Rohit 47
11. Vaibhav 50
12. Shiwali's First day of School 53
13. U-Turn 56
14. Feeling Special 59
15. An Incredible Teacher 62
16. Sleepless Nights 65
17. The Mystery of Taps 69

18.	Return Gift	72
19.	Traditional Games and Educational Value	75
20.	School Bag	78
21.	Lunch Box	81
22.	Confession	84
23.	Adaptability: A Way of Life	87
24.	Goodness: A Religion	90
25.	Happiness vs. Fitness	93
26.	Grass on the Playground	96
27.	Yes! I Am Lucky	100
28.	Music Heals ♪♪♪♪	103
29.	I Clean & …… You…	107
30.	The Liberty to a Mental Hospital	110
31.	The Magic of Appreciation	113
32.	The Titanic and Covid19	116
33.	Life Online	119
34.	Shifting Expectations	122
35.	The Unexpressed	125
36.	Good Mothers and Habits	128
37.	Our Soldiers, Our Pride	131
38.	Perfection: A Virtue	134
39.	Washrooms	137
40.	Cheerleaders	141
41.	Development vs. Deforestation	144
42.	Hmm vs Mmm	147
43.	Victim and the Culprit	150
44.	Be like Air	153

45.	One Thread Less	156
46.	Traditional Talent Hunt	159
47.	Mother Tongue and NEP	162
48.	Flying High	165
49.	Stray Animals	168
50.	Examination	171
51.	Old is Sold	174
52.	Live Your Life	176
53.	Teacher: An Entertainer	178
54.	A Burden Called Tuition Class	182
55.	My Death	185

'I Shouldn't be Alive'

This statement gives me goose bumps even today, because to imagine a situation where you can see the end of your life is actually rare and uncommon. But this had really happened to me when I was just four or five years old. My father had been transferred to Bapatla, a very small, remote coastal place and it was my mother's wish to at least visit all the places nearby before his next posting. So, the whole family along with some family friends, planned to go to Rameswaram, a very sacred place for all Hindus. We always used to be excited about any travel plans. All of us reached the place and I remember a few things that have faded in my memory but not completely erased, even if a long period of time has passed creating so many memories; some overlapped, some squeezed, some folded, and some still as fresh as if it had all just occurred yesterday.

Just before we reached the *kund* to have a holy bath, my mom and father had to go to a nearby shop to purchase materials needed to perform *pooja*. He instructed my elder sister, 'You stay here and take care of her since she is young. We will be just here at the shop.' I don't remember what exactly happened during those few minutes. I thought, since we have to have a holy bath, let us start so we can save our time too.

As we resided in a coastal area for years, all of us were aware of the ocean and its depth. I took a plunge in the water and to my surprise, the water there was very deep and I did not know how to swim. The salty water of the sea started getting into my mouth, nose, eyes, and ears. My hands were moving in all the possible directions to rescue myself or get any damn help. My legs were paddling with the best of my effort but my body was sinking, and I started to drown. I could not even scream for help because I was already in the water, and to open my mouth meant getting more water in the body again, leading to an increase in weight and sinking further.

I don't know what happened, all of a sudden, I found some structure beside me, blindly searching for a person. It was my father who was searching for his daughter desperately in that holy water because he somehow had that gut feeling. He thought, 'I am on a pilgrimage. How could I lose a member of my family?' He put his hand in the water randomly and was desperate to find his daughter. It was a very typical situation; on one hand, there was the struggle of a daughter who was sinking and on the other, a distressed father putting in the best of his abilities to search, find, rescue his lost daughter, who the water was trying to engulf. For my father, as the time passed, his hopes were sinking like the 'Titanic', but he still didn't lessen his physical efforts. All of a sudden, I could catch hold of his hand and I still remember I used all the strength of my muscles and held his arm very tightly and he left no stone unturned to pull me up and out of that water. I was hanging on his arm like a piece of cloth and he happily laid my body very gently on the floor nearby. He was full of joy for getting his daughter back before it was too late. He started gently pressing my chest and all the water started coming out. After a while, I opened my eyes and looked around. I then started crying, maybe due to happiness that I had gotten my life back. We all were happy and continued with our tour.

Although, this was not the end of adventure in life during my childhood. We then reached Swami Vivekananda Smarak, took a steamboat, and got off when we reached the remote island. The moment we got off, I started moving towards the entry without realizing that the whole family is left behind. After moving ahead for quite some time, I realized that again I was left alone. I started crying and didn't know where a lady came from and held my hand. She sat along with me near the gate thinking that everyone had to get in from here. Again, waiting was my only option. She offered me biscuits and kept consoling me that my parents would come and take me. As a child, I was too young to believe in the power of God and the faith that keeps you going when going gets tough. Swamiji's memorial is a great place. How could something like this happen here? Moreover, it is a holy place. Rameswaram is one of the *Char dhams* for Hindus. The unfortunate incidence of a child getting separated from her parents was not possible here. It was a tug-of-war between the situation and the thoughts in my mind because I re-joined the family and got lost again.

God is great, greater are the blessings we hardly realize. My family emerged in front of my eyes. My sight was blurred as the tears were floating till the brim of my small eyes, but my smile was broad and bright. My heart was pumping and jumping to see all my family members.

The feeling of insecurity and fear left me the same way darkness disappears with the spread of slight light rays; it was a divine experience. At that tender age, I learned a big lesson that my family, identity, and strength are the reasons for me to be alive. After that day, those few moments that shook me made me stronger forever.

> *'Life's battles don't always go to the stronger or faster man. But sooner or later, the man who wins is the man who thinks he can.'*

How I became a Writer

Similar to everyone else's mind, mine is also filled with thoughts, ideas, and so many things. I always feel like, if at all it were to be opened, it would be found overflowing with so many thoughts; positive, negative, useful, useless, desirable, undesirable, analytical, critical, etc. I started scribbling them on any piece of paper as an attempt to get an outlet for the volcano erupting inside my skull every time. I don't know why people like myself surprise others with the very existence of our brains and sometimes, astonish them with the excessive and extreme use of it. Such a situation puts us in a dilemma and the famous quote, 'To be or not to be, that is the question' comes to mind.

Whenever I saw students writing their paper in exams, their silence and the way they were writing tempted me to pen down a few lines and these few lines became paragraphs and the paragraphs turned in to pages. God knows! Someone once said, 'Language and grammar are important but the most important is the flow of thoughts, which should be free-flowing, effortlessly and smoothly'. I started attempting question papers, particularly in Hindi; it's my mother tongue and has always been my first love. So, I started writing in Hindi but typing and getting it published was another problem. This problem compelled me to write in English and resulted in a dual solution. I could write in both languages with the same speed and ease. It really feels very nice when you are able to translate your impulses, feelings, experiences, blueprints into scripts in words, letters, and document them. Not only for myself but for the relevance of others too.

My mind and thought process is very different and I always have seen the brighter side of every situation. I do compare anything happening around with various angles. I try to establish relationships with each and every object and hence the outcome and conclusion is totally unexpected. My language is very simple and to read the handwriting, minds, body language and behaviour of people have given me a lot of experience and knowledge. When both of these are wrapped with the right proportion of wisdom, the written matter becomes meaningful and enjoyable both. The most important among all, which has worked like a booster dose was the constant positive, encouraging feedback to whatever I wrote lengthy or short, English or Hindi……finally helped me accept myself as a writer.

My memory is also very good and tenacious. It won't let go of things easily once it's captured. At times, it gets very difficult to manage so much data, store, and segregate it properly and retrieve the relevant file as and when needed. It sets the best example of your good memory. I still remember when my friend Niloo would ask, 'How do you remember so many things?' I also then thought about the thousands of songs, many birthdays, anniversaries, movie dialogues, vehicle numbers, roll numbers, phone numbers, etc. that are stored in this small space. I feel like my mind is as strong as a hard disk with a huge storage capacity, equipped with the latest microprocessor to process data at the speed of sound. I wouldn't say at the speed of light because it is not that fast.

Sometimes, penning down all this information and getting the proper words to express them is more than enough. At times, even my students and children get surprised that I remember so many events in such a detailed way. This might be due to heredity; my mother also had a very great memory. She always surprised us with this special attribute of hers.

"If we did the things we are capable of, we would astound ourselves".

My First Class

I still remember it was a post half-yearly exam day. I was introduced to the students of sixth standard, a class of thirty-seven students on the fourth floor of the school. It was beside the computer room. The moment I entered, I was welcomed by the students. They greeted me and sat quietly because they were trying to get to know me and I was doing the same. There was a complete shift in my attitude because I was teaching undergraduates, postgraduates, and even corporates in a computer institute, which I left to join the school as a teacher.

Reaching here was not an easy task at all. Few of my friends forced me to appear for this post in the school. I too thought there is no harm in trying, giving interviews is one of my hobbies. So, I appeared for the interview, a huge panel of six great personalities were waiting to bombard their questions on me. I too was well prepared and was equipped with 90 percent of self-confidence and 10 percent was my subject knowledge, communication skills, dressing up, appearance, presence of mind and of course a bright smile. After qualifying the interview, I was again called for a demonstration in a class, then again, a final round of interview and then I was given this responsibility.

I was a lean, short-height girl who was supposed to take up the responsibility of these angels. I liked the atmosphere of the school because we were given the freedom to deal with the children in any way that is good for them. It was more of a learning experience for me than teaching because I was supposed to maintain registers, documents, test papers, notebook corrections and a record of each and every child. I was also trying to meet all the deadlines and be punctual. My sincerity and integrity helped me come out of this very easily.

I started teaching them science; it was like I was changing my 'software' because to move from teaching computers to science was a shift. Actually, it can be considered a double shift, since it was both a change in the grade and subject as well. Gradually, I started learning, studying, analyzing, and taking care of the needs of the children. We became friends. Whenever anybody asked, 'Which grade are you the class teacher of?' I replied, 'Six-D'. To which they often said, 'Oh my God! Okay, that notorious, rowdy, undisciplined class'. I never liked my students being labelled by these terms because I always believed, beauty lies in the eyes of the beholder and what you do gets reflected. I taught them science in a manner that I liked and I simply loved them unconditionally, and this love, affection, and care transformed all those children into real angels. They started behaving well, studying well, became dreamy, and ambitious. I was touched when I saw some of them preparing handmade cards with lovely messages, which may have wrong grammar and incorrect spelling but the approach was straight from their hearts. I realized my importance and responsibility. There were only a few months to pass and all my students passed out in flying colours.

The Principal was very surprised that this inexperienced girl could handle such a difficult class so nicely without a single complaint reaching her and that all the so-called issues were solved within the four walls of the class. I loved the students so much that if they did anything wrong, they would come up on their own and admit it, feel sorry, and promise that it won't get repeated. What else do you want? All the parents were so happy with such the positive approach and the new way of handling students that after summer vacations, I got allotted the very same students for another year. They were happy and I was too. I can still hear them screaming out of joy when they saw me coming to the class as their class teacher again.

'A positive thinker creates a majority.'

The Haunting Backstage

We used to have a cultural week as part of a huge cultural fest, in which the basic mantra was that every child must have a stage performance. This is usually done at the school-level because small children hardly realize the magnitude of the task they are doing or that is done. Once they learn, it becomes easy for them to climb any stage at any stage of their lives; without even realizing what stage fear is, they emerge out as winners. Some students are full of talent, some may not even know their latent abilities. This difficult task is done by teachers and the outcome surprises both the parents and the students.

With this mindset, various cultural activities are organized in this four-day mega fest. I was in-charge of invocation and we were supposed to select and train the students with the help of dance teachers. At the end of everything, you may end up becoming a dance teacher or even forget what your actual subject expertise is. Anyway, that particular year we decided to invoke the Sun, the ultimate source of energy. We began our practice and everything went on smoothly. Since it was a co-education school, we had to select both boys and girls in equal proportion or balance. There was just a day left for our final performance, and I know the closer you are to D-Day, the madder you'd become. You'd start behaving like a transformer that is overloaded and trips every now and then. I sat with the participants and started distributing costumes to them. It was a tedious task because along with the clothes, a lot of ornaments were also given. I did everything in a very systematic and meticulous manner. A child was absent and his costume was with me.

The next day, our performance was at 12:30 PM. I had called the student participants to the allotted rooms at around 11:00 AM. Most of them were punctual, but the child that was absent came around 11:30 AM. The moment I saw him, I got the opportunity to let my anxiety strain out. I lectured him and his father. The father was a real gentleman who heard everything and was still calm. I handed over the costume pack and asked him to get ready. The father helped the child get dressed. After a few minutes, when I started the final headcount to confirm if all the students were ready, this fellow was hiding in the corner. I raised my voice and called him closer for the final check. The child approached me in a very hesitant manner and my anger sublimed. I started smiling and then laughing. I held the child and apologised, as I had handed over a girl's costume to him in a hurry and tension, but he wore it quickly and was ready. I loved this. We then quickly replaced his costume. The performance was awesome; we got the prize, but even today the backstage still haunts me!

The simple reason being, all that glitters on stage is due to the team burning the midnight oil behind the scene. The passion, art, ambition, love, and dedication to put the best foot forward is everything that is needed. The audience must have an everlasting experience. All the hard work, tension, anxiety, conflicts, differences in opinion, and fights fade away when you are declared the winner and you are paid well for all the madness.

'The difference between ordinary and extraordinary is that little extra'.

Emotional Connection

I read somewhere that a teacher's job is so special because it connects them to a child and their parents, and the affection developed remains for a long time. Teaching is a profession in which you are actually dealing with the most important resource and its management i.e., human resources. What you invest today in the form of love, care, guidance, training, and character building will surely bear the fruits of tomorrow and will lead to a healthy society; includes meeting physical, mental, social, and emotional needs and well-being.

Humans are so different; they not only have external differences but internal ones that are more complicated and at times, unpredictable. Parents also don't know their children well. In most of the *PTM*, the usual occurrence is that parents visit the teachers and receive complaints about their child from them. I always felt that PTM are not just for complaining, and something more positive and constructive could be done, or at least the parents need to be taken in private and worked with in solving the difficulty. A teacher can do this in a much simpler way because they have handled so many students and have wider experience but the parents are the ones who may have one, two, or three children at most.

The first thing is to help parents learn about their own children, second is looking for better and more positive characteristics of the child, then informing the child what they are good at, and trying to polish those skills to help them become the best at it. As I always say, it would require less time and energy to make strong things stronger than a weak one.

Sometimes, your kind words, timely help, and a bit of guidance can do wonders. In the meeting, parents should be made to feel good about their child and not guilty. Try to look at the child from their parent's eyes, your problems become simpler and solvable. Never ever create a concrete, rigid image of any child because in their case, I always say, 'The first impression is not the last impression'. There has to be room to accept positive changes to see growth in these children. Sometimes parents happen to meet you with the mindset to hear only complaints, since the previous three or four teachers they would have met only shared negative remarks about their child.

You can surprise them by changing their mind with some positive strokes. Make them realize that they are the parents of a child; the best gift one can have. The child is normal and healthy, growing and developing naturally. The child listens, obeys, has a gentle, sweet heart, is helpful, kind, honest, completes their work, etc. After all this, the room for improvement is understood, but if you make a huge heap of negativity and then ask to search for the good it will result in tension, stress, and frustration. Connect with the parent and child emotionally. Understand that you have a huge responsibility and a magic wand too; use it wisely and timely before it is too late.

Let the parents have pride in having the child and not pain. They already have a lot to think about, do, and support. Do not shirk the responsibility. If you are capable of leaving even a small positive impact, just do it.

"Respect other people if you want to be respected".

Attention

When you study human psychology, you find so many facts and myths. It's not necessary that all facts are true for every individual. We are born with so many differences and abilities. We have a habit of analyzing and preparing our minds before actually knowing something. This preoccupied mind creates too many problems.

We give importance to physical appearance, what someone is wearing, how they look, how they're carrying themselves and after all this analysis, we approach them. As a teacher, when you get to any class to teach, if you go with such a mental preparation, then you will never be successful in delivering the best to be able to get the best outcome. In fact, the moment you enter the class, the full strength of the class must connect with you and each child should feel that you are their teacher. If you are able to achieve this, then rest become a cakewalk.

It so happened, a few months back that one of my students walked into school and was searching for me desperately to meet. Ultimately, he found me in the Knowledge Centre. I was not in a good mood that day. I was upset on my own yet completing my work. The child saw me and came running and touched my feet. I blessed him and very casually asked about his whereabouts with the least interest. I knew what I was doing was wrong but I couldn't overcome it. Then, I offered him a chair, he sat, and then we had a little chat. I started murmuring out my negativity and told him that I wanted to leave school now and that it is such a thankless job. No one bothers how good you are or what your contributions are. There is no acknowledgment and recognition. I am not enjoying it the way I used to. To my surprise, the child simply heard everything and stayed calm. He somehow knew that his teacher wasn't in her usual senses but then, what he said changed me completely.

He said, 'Mam please look at me, you remember how I used to look in class? Small, lean, dark in complexion, timid, under-confident boy. Do you know mam, you were the reason I came to school every day. No one until that standard ever paid attention to me and it was you whose period I would wait for desperately. I used to think to myself, "Now mam will come, she will look at me, talk to me, appreciate and motivate me in front of all the students in the class." Do you know mam, that was the time when this student of yours had broken his cocoon of being under-confident? I pursued your subject—biology and I am doing research on stem cells in Belgium. Please, mam, promise me, you will never leave the school because you will never know, in which class a child like me is waiting to be transformed and only you can be the reason for him to attend school and feel good about himself.' I was so emotional; tears rolled down my cheek and I thought this is the reflection of attention that was given to him. Like an ECG graph, there are ups and downs in life.

Every professional faces it often, but after this I realized, whenever the line is down, we must wait for some time and it will surely bounce back and move upward.

'Attitude is much more important than aptitude'.

Anger and Laughter

A good teacher is one who has very good control over his or her emotions, sentiments, and feelings. If you know how to quickly switch these off at any moment, there is nothing like it. The reason is, the situations happening in the class, where you coordinate and respond, are so temporary that you can't presume that the first impression will be the last. They may certainly change but if you create a concrete image about any child, circumstance, or parent, then it will be a problem for everyone, in the long run.

I am not saying you should not be angry; one should be if the situation demands for it but the moment things come back to normal, you must also be cool. There were quite a few situations when my anger suddenly got converted into laughter. I can compare it to a *dosa* tawa; when a dosa tawa is very hot, the water that is sprinkled on it will bring the temperature down to what is needed. All the nine *rasas* of emotions must be used extensively, if you wish to be the best teacher.

I still remember, I was just calling out the marks of the students to recheck the entries in my register. There was a boy who was brainy but could never focus because his attention was distributed to so many activities happening around. I shouted and called him. He was very well behaved and with a blink of an eye, he was near me. I saw his marks, he really scored very well. Now, I was awestruck. I have already shouted. I called him close and then in the sweetest, softest happy voice I said, 'Dear child, how can you do this? You had scored very poor marks initially but now you're scoring such good marks'. He gave me a surprised look, thinking I was playing a game with him. I reassured him saying, 'Please tell everyone what made you do this. I am so happy for you, seriously'. Then he said, 'Madam, you have always told me that I can perform well. This statement was ringing in my head constantly. I thought to myself, that if you are saying this, then let me try at least once and I tried'. I was very happy and I started respecting the child.

In another instance, I called a child for writing a note in his school diary about his behaviour, out of my curiosity, I started reading the personal information on the page beside. I was very angry at that time but while reading, there was a column for information about the house (this is the house assigned by the school to students for inter-house activities), but it was misinterpreted by the parents and they wrote bungalow. There was a sudden spurt of laughter; that one word had completely changed my anger into laughter. I didn't write a note in his diary and instead gave him a piece of simple personal advice, which is more effective than giving notes in the diary at times.

This is the beauty of the teaching profession, you deal with so many wonderful, adventurous, uniquely different individuals. We can't have a single yardstick to measure the differences and we must realise, accept, and respect each of them. All are different, all are important!

'Everything has its beauty but not everyone sees it'.

Picnic and Panic

It was a pleasant winter morning just after our Christmas vacations. We headed for our class picnic to a nearly thirty-five km picnic spot called Ramdham. Since they were fifth standard students, we had the list of all the students along with their parent's contact number, travel plan, and everything in place; it was a very meticulously designed activity. All the students reported at around 6:30 AM, we started our journey by 7:15 AM, after a simple pooja. The ride was filled with screams of excitement, songs, colourful caps, stylish sunglasses, and bags full of favourite snacks. We all got inside the allotted buses and with a proper headcount, we began to move. So many songs, new and old, *Antakshari*, Bollywood-Hollywood, jokes, and whatnot. The whole process was a small compartment filled with extreme energy and bubbly young talents. Till the bus reached its destination, the enthusiasm had no end and when we reached, all of them got off. There were guides to divide the children into groups and take them in a properly planned manner without too much of hustle and bustle at one place. Children were briefed and asked to behave well and take care of themselves and their fellow mates.

I had one juvenile diabetic girl student who was supposed to take her insulin injection before lunch. By then, my class came near the game zone and they all started playing. Seeing them enjoying and having a lot of fun, I took this girl to a separate place to have her injection. As we returned to the game zone, came a huge shock of my life, one of the students fell and fractured his forearm. Being a science teacher, I knew that the forearm has two bones radio-ulna. But I never thought I would see it like this in the arms of one of my students. The sight was beyond description; the bone was broken and completely out of the flesh at both ends. I couldn't believe my eyes; such a thing has never happened before. My senior colleague was there with me; the manager and our physical education teacher joined us and within no time, we decided to take the child for first-aid. We tied the bone with a *dupatta*, arranged for a jeep, and went to a nearby town Ramtek, in search of an Orthopaedic Doctor and we got one. The doctor was kind enough to attend to the child immediately. He gave him a painkiller and then, a proper first-aid. In the meantime, we contacted the parents and informed them. To convey such a message to the parents who were so far away and will need at least an hour to reach this place was another difficult task. My senior and I were with the ten-years-old child who was so strong to have tolerated all the pain very gracefully, like a warrior. He was not blaming anyone and very humbly admitted his own mistake. His parents reached the spot at the speed of light; they were happy to see that child with proper first-aid. Being his class teacher, I decided to accompany them back and so, we started our return journey. He was very calm and cool because his parents were also good and understood the whole situation. We took the child to a good child Orthopaedic Surgeon and he performed the surgery. I was with the parents throughout and then, when the doctor gave us the sign that everything was under-control, the parents made arrangements to drop me to school, as my two-wheeler was parked there. For the first time, I became so tense and could feel the adrenaline rush in my body, it was not letting me calm down. I reached home, took a fresh bath, sat in front of God, and prayed. I expressed my gratitude, 'Thank you, God. You are always there to save all of us'.

After a few days, I made a home visit to meet the child. He was well; his family became more of a friend after that incidence. In between, we also had a class photograph for which I requested his parents to bring him; they did and that was a night I could not sleep as I kept thinking over and again about how a nice school picnic ended in a panic.

This incident gave me a lesson for life—any trip, journey, or event we may take up, or have planned, make it fool-proof. Even so, accidents are undetectable surprises waiting for us. So, the presence of mind and our heart helps us deal with such a situation. One must always take care and let the pain sublime, leaving the memory to be cherished throughout.

'Living is the art of getting used to what we didn't expect'.

Out-of-the-Box Techniques

When your mind thinks of newer things, ideas, ways, solutions to problems, or even starts establishing relationships between a concept and its application, then an actual learning has taken place. Most of the time we acquire knowledge through books, our parents, teachers, friends and so many other sources in the digital world but until you use it, utilize it, and apply it, it actually remains incomplete. In other words, it is difficult to teach a concept convincingly until you help the student understand why it has to be learned, where it is used, and leave this question in the mind of the child—'Where can I use it to help reduce labor, time, and energy?'

This not only quenches but still leaves hunger to explore the world the way they wish to do. I always told children, 'Dear students, I don't love my subject. I live it every day, every moment and that's why anyone can ask me any doubt, at any anytime'. This is the policy I have followed for years. When children see you practicing what you preach, they start believing you, trust you, and then follow you. Following does not mean losing their identity. They should be like the stars in the sky; all glowing, shining with their own light, without getting affected and being compared. For all this, you need to perform experiments and my subject does them a lot. I have always kept my imagination and the real thing separate, which means something that is to be imagined must be, but something that can be easily seen, felt, or made available should never be imagined.

I used this technique of imagination while teaching them about different types of habitats. I would ask all of them to close their eyes, and then, narrate something that they will listen to and try to imagine. This helps in developing the power of imagination; every child has the freedom to imagine the way they wish to, yet the objective remains common.

Writing letters—I have always given importance to those who are the silent kind, and do not have the habit of speaking, or asking anything. The reason being, silent students should never be taken lightly because they are also an integral part of the class. For such children, writing a letter to their class teacher is the best way to express, since there are no specifications and limits. Speaking their heart out is more important than anything. It's no wonder these students have really surprised me with their great insights, they believe in the power of observation.

I also used my one-liners very effectively, these were liked by all my students. Most of them are well remembered by my students even today; out of all those, some were phrases, thoughts, and some created by yours truly. For example, being a science teacher, drawing diagrams is an integral part of written work and tests, it has to be appropriately labelled too so, I would say 'A diagram without a label is like a TV without cable', or other phrases like, 'Satisfaction is the death of progress', 'There is a hairline difference between being extraordinary and abnormal', 'Learn to appreciate whole-heartedly', 'Clap loudly for others', 'Stay happy and spread happiness', 'Be honest, you will be rare and unique', etc.

Home work for habit—Present-day children are very fussy about their food and are more fascinated with junk food rather than home-cooked fresh food. They make faces of disagreement, feel sad, or even show anger. The whole purpose and good effects of food is lost if there is a fight for acceptance. So, I gave them homework, for at least a week's time, whatever was served to them at home, they were to say, 'Wow!', and eat their food. I asked them to see the happiness on the face of their mothers and grandmothers, to surprise them. I asked them to try eating all the things that they always said no to, with the probability that the food tastes good and it's only their thinking that made it like this. How could I forget the child who literally grew potatoes when I taught them about vegetative propagation? Since potatoes are a perennial crop, the next year, he made it a point to meet me and bring French fries that were made from the potatoes he grew. He said 'Mam, so many potatoes could be grown with a single eye of a potato'. The happiness and the learnings he got was huge and for lifetime. The same happened to me too.

Once a week, all the students were asked to obey whatever is said to them in school, at home; irrespective of who was saying, the point was to just listen and do it as this improves our listening skills, helps being modest, obedient and the person whom you obey starts respecting you for this gesture. Later, if you need any help, they will be ready to lend you a helping hand without having any hesitation.

'Cultivation to the mind is as necessary as food to the body'.

Rohit

We all still remember the movie *'Koi Mil Gaya'* and Rohit, a child with special needs who actually becomes special because of the power blessed by an Alien (*Jadu*). This is a story of such a Rohit in my school. I still remember, when I handled a substitution period for one of the first standard classes, I met this lean, smart boy, fair with twinkling eyes, very enthusiastic, and energetic. His class teacher had told me that he is a real hero. I looked at her in a surprising manner. She asked me to have a look at his hand, I got the shock of my life; at every joint, there was a surgery performed to make his immovable joints move. A child, just six years of age, had already borne these painful situations because of his health.

Rohit was blessed with extra special parents, who along with his elder brother, did every possible thing to make him an independent individual. Today, I see so many who are healthy physically yet have a mind of a sick person, but Rohit was the opposite; if you just look at his face, no one can even imagine what he has undergone. Days and years passed. He was always interested in science and would always come up with certain ideas. He would search for me at school, make it a point to tell me about his great ideas. Then I would explain then again, he would add something and had a never-give-up attitude.

He always wanted to participate in science model-making competitions. Then came '*Avishkar*' at Priyadarshini College of Engineering. Rohit was in ninth standard. He explained to me that we can easily open an umbrella at the press of a button but in order to close it, we have to pull it with a lot of effort. He said 'People like me face great difficulty, so I have made a hands-free version in which the umbrella would fold at the press of a button'. This was his own creation made to solve the problem he faced while closing the umbrella.

One should have seen Rohit, he was a boy who was very excited, happy, full of energy, and positivity. He wanted to showcase his ideas and the output to all, including the judges and prove that the disability of his body has actually added extra ability to his brain. Rohit's body language was very confident. Post-lunch, after the judges and guests visited the exhibition, we were asked to assemble in the Auditorium. All of us occupied the chairs. The best part of any ceremony is the valedictory function for the prize-distribution ceremony.

In the category that Rohit belonged to, he bagged the second prize. It was the first time for him to participate and win, something for which he had been waiting since long. He was confident but couldn't believe the announcement, he stood so quickly as if there was a spring under him and then he waited for me to join him. I held his hand. The moment we started marching towards the stage, one by one, all of the people in the Auditorium stood up and applauded; there was a thunder of claps. I can still hear it… It was amazing. There were tears flowing down my cheeks, of happiness and contentment for selecting Rohit to compete as he proved to be the right choice. When the intentions are right, the result and outcome also turn out right. God bless Rohit! He is doing so well in the field of Astrophysics in a renowned college. Happy to know you dear.

> *'Take time to be aware; it is the opportunity to help others'.*

Vaibhav

It was January, just after New year's celebration, we were supposed to represent our school in the CBSE Regional Science Exhibition in Mumbai. I was the only teacher with my team of two girl students from seventh standard. They were very good, obedient, and sincere. They always obeyed whatever was told to them. We reached Mumbai station. From there, we decided to take the local and reach our final destination—Airoli. Along with us were another team from our branch; Ashti and a male teacher with two teams of four students. Whenever we go to a science exhibition, there is always more luggage than hands. On the platform, we could always hire porters but what do we do once we have boarded the local train? A feeling of anxiety, excitement, fear, adventure, and so many other feelings were mixed up like a typical *Saoji chooda* (a Maharashtrian hot crispy snack). Since my face always reflects what my mind is thinking, like a mirror, my feelings are often predictable, true, and crystal clear; I just cannot hide them. In a jam-packed compartment, I was just calculating and planning how to get off the train in six seconds.

I am not a very religious person but have a strong faith in the Almighty. Whenever, I am in a tough situation in life that I don't have control over or when I feel helpless, I just pray and God has always answered them. I have had so many experiences in my life where a problem arises and the solution and blessings of God followed like the flash of a lightning and the roar of a thunder. I am so thankful for everything. Vaibhav was one such human being who appeared like the flash of a lightning during a gloomy moment of uncertainty.

Mumbai and local trains are inseparable; to understand which local takes you where, and through which route is not so easy. We all were waiting on the platform and were anxiously looking for a connecting local train. We used the best of our knowledge and intelligence; we read all the boards for information regarding this. We saw one arrive, with the help of the students, we boarded the train with so many big luggage, small bags, and cartons. All of a sudden, a Mumbaikar approached, maybe he could sense our hollow confidence, he asked, 'Where do you all wish to go?' We told him our destination. He immediately said 'No, no…this is going in the opposite direction'. Again, with a lot of tension, we brought all of our luggage back to the platform and counted them all to confirm. We did this foolish exercise thrice until we got the correct local train that took us to the desired destination.

Although this was not done deliberately, our mixed feelings of excitement, tension with a pinch of foolishness, and a lot of ignorance was enjoyed. These incidences actually teach us to appreciate our idiotic behavior and how to rectify them before it's too late. This is how learning by doing or experiential learning occurs.

Now came the short interval during which we were supposed to get off the train; just six seconds and more than eight bags including suitcases, cartons, other things in a new place with two delicate girls. I don't know where a boy, who looked like he was in his late-twenties appeared from, he said 'Mam, you get down with the girls and I will drop all your luggage quickly'. We got off and before I could realize, all of us were safely placed on the platform with each and every bag. When I looked up, after confirming the number of bags, the local had already moved. I shouted and asked, 'What's your name, dear?' to which he replied, 'Vaibhav'. I murmured so many blessings and good wishes that day. His bright, smiling face, and the attitude to help has etched a memory in my brain's hard-disk that can never be erased and will always be cherished.

Whenever I am not able to do anything for anyone or feel helpless, it's my habit to bless, pray, and wish for the best things to happen in their lives. These wishes, although invisible and non-materialistic, have tremendous power to change a dream into reality. Thank you, God, for sending an angel named Vaibhav.

'Good actions give strength to ourselves and inspire good actions in others'.

Shiwali's First day of School

It was my then three-year-old daughter, Shiwali's first day of nursery school. Me and my husband, both being teachers, left for school early in the morning. I kept her uniform, shoes, socks, handkerchief, bag, tiffin-box, and a water bottle ready with her aunt who took care of her. The aunt is more of a family friend than a caretaker. We share a strong bond of love. I also fixed a van person who dropped her to the school. As a working person, I had to sacrifice so many small vital moments of my life, in order to add great moments to other's lives. With the confidence that I have done everything, I reached the school. At around 10:30 AM, I realized that she must have reached the school too. The pre-primary building is separate. It was my free period, so like any mother, I rushed to see my daughter in school uniform on the very first day of her school life. I had to take a secret glance at her, otherwise she would get distracted or may wish to come along. The moment I reached the grill, I stood beside the wall to at least take a glance at my little angel.

Most of the small children were crying; some were crying for no reason because they could see their classmates crying. Some were giving a funny look wondering, 'What is this place? Why are so many of us trapped in these four walls?' Some were the philosophical kind, their expression said, 'Oh my God! There are so many others like me; all wearing the same clothes with no variety'. Some were reluctant about everything happening; they were lost in their own worlds. Many were standing near the doorway to look at their parents or grandparents. In between gazing at all these children, I realized the purpose of me standing there. I saw among all the students standing in the corridor, only one student had worn improper uniform i.e., the side which was supposed to be at the back was in front and vice-versa. Her back was towards me, the child was neatly dressed but in a wrong manner. A proper hairdo—a small pony like a fountain just above the forehead with a small fresh *mogra* flower. I started smiling, thinking to myself about how these days, parents are overly excited about everything in regard to their children. Suddenly, the child turned. Oh God! I got the shock of my life. It was my own daughter, Shiwali, who was wearing the improper uniform. I immediately called the support staff of her class and asked them to do the needful. She agreed and very politely said, "I was also thinking, but now I will do it".

It was then that I realized how sometimes a tense situation ends up becoming a memory forever. I still cherish that moment with her aunt who is now a very close friend of mine. My friend Renu who accompanied me said 'Look how beautifully the aunt has gotten her ready for school. Tomorrow onwards, you should ask her to get you ready for school too'. This way, the first day of school became more memorable for me and Shiwali. When I came home, I narrated the whole thing to her aunt to which she replied very innocently, 'My husband and I had a discussion for around thirty minutes as to what was the correct way of wearing the uniform and ultimately, it still went wrong'. What a beautiful memory!

> *"Life is a succession of lessons which must be lived to be understood".*

U-Turn

I received a call, late in the evening from a school authority who clearly stated that I have to take up the class teacher ship of a new class in between an on-going session. I was left with no option and my mind unknowingly started to think about so many things; the why, who, when, what, etc. of the situation. The next morning, I was called and all the documents of the new class were handed over to me and I became their class teacher overnight. When you replace somebody, particularly at a school-level, in between an on-going session, all eyes of the students are on you. Their eyes work like X-ray machines that try to penetrate deep, think and get the right answer to the questions they have in mind. It was one of the most difficult times of my life; I was looked at as a person who'd hopefully bring positive changes but at the same time, I asked myself then, 'Why? Why is this done?'

It was with my churning emotions, sentimentality, love, affection, and empathy that I had to take care of a child who developed a hatred not only for his school but also his life. An innocent child, just ten-years-old, was struggling every day to avoid school time. After school hours, he forgot everything and wished to live only in the safe confined area, his home. I started thinking about how to solve this. When you deal with children, you have to be extra careful because while trying to manage certain issues, we may cause damage beyond repair. I called his parents. They were very supportive and told me that they'd cooperate with what I wished and decided to do. Now I was fully ready, as the authorities were there to support me and had given me the freedom, at the same time the parents were also confident about me. My work began. Every day after reaching the school, I would check for his attendance, if he wasn't present, I called his parents to speak to the child. Finally, he started turning up twice a week. I rigorously followed up, then it increased to three times a week. The day he was in class, I would visit the class a number of times, with reason or without, just to have a glance at his activities and behavior. I made a small team of students who would constantly be with him and reported to me at the end of the day. I selected him as a part of CCA activities. Since he was given work that he was interested in, he attended school and did them. His notebook completion was also taken care of by some caring children including some girls. Then, in November when we had cultural week, I gave him a very important role. He performed it so well and received a best performance award.

Slowly, I motivated him to study too. He became regular, good study-wise, participative, friendly, helpful, and most importantly, he could break that invisible barrier he created in his mind out of fear. He took the U-turn needed for his life and all the negativity vanished.

Again, next year I was given his class teachership and I tried my level best to do whatever I could. At times, no awards or no rewards can certify what you have done. On the last report card day, his father came much earlier than the usual time, sat in front of me, the tears in his eyes said it all. He said, 'Madam, I do not have any words that can actually express what I have to say to you. Today when I look at my child, I can see your tireless efforts which I can never forget as a parent. May God bless you!' I too became emotional because an act done straight from the heart can never be done artificially. It does take honest efforts, selfless thoughts, and a very positive approach.

No one can understand the bond between me and the child. Even today, in a group of teachers if he looks at me, the eyes say it all. No one can explain why and no one can ask why not.

At times, as teachers, your emotions get so exhausted but like a well, they reflow and keep the warmth and affection alive.

"Have a heart that never hardens, and a temper that never tries, and a touch that never hurts".

Feeling Special

I have read a thought, 'We may forget about the conversations we have had, but never forget how a person made you feel'. These children are really sweet and innocent. They just wish to have a place in the class, some friends, the teacher's attention, a healthy atmosphere and a lot of fun. I still remember, when I used to go to junior classes, students would quickly draw something, write a short simple message, do a bit of colouring using crayons, and sweetly hand it over to you. The point is not what is written and drawn or how it is made, but the child spending his time, taking the pain, and making you feel special.

Similarly, I know that every Teacher's Day, *Guru Poornima*, or my birthday, etc., the students will do so much; they will get cards, flowers, handmade artefacts, and simple letters. They will decorate the classroom and share some of their rare feelings. Every year, I get many flowers, cards, messages, and small handmade gifts. All this has really contributed a lot in me growing, developing, and learning to be better. I kept changing my plans, strategies, teaching techniques, surprising them, and even thought out-of-the-box at times. I did this to give importance to the child and have a child-centred way of teaching.

One fine day I realised, when my student writes something about me and gives me gifts I feel so special;

what if I do it the same for the whole class, particularly the one I am a class teacher of? This began and now every Children's day, I do something that makes my students feel special. When I was the class teacher of lower classes, I would walk up to every child's desk and give them a rose, shake their hands, and wish them. When I became the class teacher of a higher class, I wrote a citation for each and every student about their special and positive attributes. This not only makes them feel special but it acts as a booster. They can keep the citations with them, read it again, and get motivated or encouraged to get better or at least move on. If a small child can make you feel good, then why can't we reciprocate and react in a more positive manner? For the even more higher-class students, I selected short books written by Swami Vivekananda and gifted it along with a handwritten citation. Each and every one read them. They felt happy and excited to have something that their class teacher had done that no one else has. It's like Newton's third law of motion—For every action, there is an equal and opposite reaction. If you want to feel good, happy, motivated and special, give all that to children, what you get in return would be like compound interest and much more than your imagination. It doesn't always take too much for me or anyone to feel special. It could mean having the patience to wait ten or twenty minutes after school hours to discuss with the parents or students; that can also be fulfilling as it could be the turning point of one's life. If a few minutes of your day can change someone else's whole life then no dividend can be better than that. As time passes, what stays in your mind is how you made the child feel by taking the initiative to stay back and help them in the best possible way and how that one step made their life a cakewalk. It is really important that these children come back to school after many years and search for you. This search of theirs is not of just love, but a deep-rooted love.

"Life without love is like a tree without blossom and fruit".

An Incredible Teacher

Imagine you're a teacher and a trainee student is sitting at the driver's seat; the timid soul has all the controls in their hands. They are yet to gain confidence but have put the ignition on and are about to make the turn to a busy road. You are sitting beside them without any control and a fearful mind but a confident heart is murmuring prayers for the safety of both and others on the road to avoid any unfavourable circumstance or mishap. Still, instead of showing any fear, anger, or doubt, you are constantly motivating and boosting the confidence to express your faith that says, 'Yes you can do it! You will be able to do it. It's not difficult for you, I know you very well.' Faith is the only thing that works in an invisible manner but its result is loud and visible. A teacher who can put their life in danger to give a student the strength of being worthy of doing what was once thought impossible, is a sign of an extraordinary teacher. Yes! I am talking about a simple man, a driver who has taught driving a car to many ladies in our city.

In our country, even today, driving is considered a task that suits only men. Before a woman learns how to drive, people say so many things without any logic like—women drive recklessly, they cannot control the vehicle properly, etc. No one, including one's family members and their spouse, is interested in them learning how to drive a car. Doubting the capabilities of a woman is a thought that percolates year after year and generation after generation. It is actually more the case of not accepting women doing all this. There are some, who talk about women empowerment and so much more, I want to tell them that women are born powerful, skilful, and tough; just give them an opportunity and they will leave you surprised and shocked at all times, in all fields.

Some smart teachers can see the potential in a student that even the parents could not see or even think of. I remember one such teacher of my daughter's from when she was in fourth standard. For the cultural celebration, it was compulsory for all students to participate. My daughter went to English Drama practice room and was given the role of a plant; silent and stable. She was happy about that so I didn't say anything because if the child is happy, I should be happy. After a week-long practice, suddenly, a teacher started searching particularly for her and scolded her saying, 'What are you doing here? I want you to be a lead singer for *qawwali*'. It was very difficult for me to digest, but interfering with the teacher's decision somehow did not feel right. Finally, the practice started and the qawwali was *'Pal do pal ka saath hamara…'*, a long difficult all-time favorite song, now I was more tense and worried.

On the final day, after the announcements, the curtain began to roll up. I had butterflies in my stomach and I was praying. The first *aalap* of the qawwali was sung by her and my heart, as a mother, started jumping. I could neither believe my eyes nor my ears, and tears rolling down my cheeks were enough to express my feelings. My daughter is such a good singer, who can perform fearlessly in front of hundreds of audiences. I was shocked that third and fourth standard students were singing this difficult piece. It was beyond my imagination but it was the hard work of a great teacher backstage which appeared like a cakewalk for the children on the stage. The performance was over, all the children got off the stage and went to their parents. They didn't even know what they had done, in terms of their wonderful performance; I think this is innocence. During the prize distribution function, one must have seen the glow on the face of a dedicated, great teacher who knew they would emerge as winners and the result was as predicted. As she walked towards the stage with all her participants, it was incredible…the *shamyana* was echoing with claps to greet the teacher, show respect, and gratitude for her hard work. Such memories can never be erased.

The words or acts of encouragement and motivation work more than miracles in anyone's life and that could be the turning point of their life. I can never forget these incredible teachers Raju bhaiya, and Mrs. Shrivastava

We should always acknowledge the efforts of such selfless teachers who see beyond the 'normal vision' and bow down with gratitude for having the ability to 'transform'.

'Nothing stands in front of a willing heart and strong determination'.

Sleepless Nights

Dr. APJ Abdul Kalam ji has rightly said that if we put the right proportion of the 3Hs—Head, Hand, and Heart in something, we make masterpieces. This has a great impact on an ordinary person like myself, who is passionate about whatever is done. Be it a simple act of mopping floors, washing utensils, or even drawing *rangoli,* or preparation for any competition for students as participants or for myself as a contestant. We do not win instantaneously; we have to learn the proper approach, attitude, and put in a lot of hard work with a perfect blend of confidence, neither too less nor more. When all these are in place, only then can you think of finding a place on the victory stand. It is rightly said, 'Winners don't do different things. They do things differently'.

Those who understand and develop this temperament of a winner, will eventually grow and start winning. If a certain stage is reached, winning becomes your habit. I am no exception to this whole process; as a science teacher, I have to prepare students for exhibitions, talks, quizzes and so many other competitions including singing, drama, speeches, etc. My hands are always full with such competitions. I always enjoyed these because I take them as opportunities to learn something new. In the present-day situation, resources are more the originality of the concept and its application becomes rare. This is because, for every small problem, idea, concept, presentation, or a simple question, every individual has a simple solution which is to search it on the internet. This net, as the name suggests, is an excellent example of making anyone look busy or keeping them engaged without any substantial output. A person may have spent their whole day and the end result would just be hollow.

I always tell my students and friends to have the internet be the last option. First, you should forcibly let your brain think. Psychology says this process will surely help come out with a great unique idea. Secondly, whatever is on the net, belongs to everyone; anyone can access it from anywhere, anytime. If this is done, explore relevant books from a library or conduct a brainstorming session with the students then, excellent results that surprises everyone can be expected. Our brains are made up of cells which when exerted and tired becomes more creative in its approaches. It has to be trained to think in a way that helps you achieve desired results. The more we use it, the sharper and quicker it becomes. It is rightly said that a computer can do the jobs of fifty people but the fifty computers can never do the job done by an extraordinary mind. So, when the power of imagination is mixed with creativity, the outcome is immense satisfaction.

Once I know that I have a task to perform, my mind automatically gets so involved that it only thinks about it all-day and night, until I start getting solutions or ideas to execute. In this process of tension, I have lost count of how many nights I couldn't sleep due to this creative, inquisitive, explorative research-based thinking. Then, to finally draw a plan to execute will take away the sleep of a few more nights. Ultimately, we began with a lot of paperwork, photographs, documentation, registration, and whatnot. The extreme pressure of having to perform the best, receive fair judgement, present well, and to win is always there in the back of my mind. So many prayers, *mantras, tantras, totkas,* etc. will be performed simultaneously in a discreet manner because science doesn't believe in it but I do. The dawn of the final day entails getting all decked up with every necessary thing from a pin to glue guns, and carrying them to be transported. This included ensuring we have laptops, write-ups, identity cards, proper uniforms, Bonafede certificates, registration forms, money, exhibit models properly packed and that our tension is covered with a confident smile. The last thing to be done while preparing for a competition is arranging everything in the allotted place, doing a final check, blessing and wishing the students, preparing them to take up any challenges that can test their inner strengths, presence of mind, and knowledge. After the judgements, at most times, the valedictory functions take place post-lunch; even today it gives me goosebumps of excitement and nervousness.

Assembling in the hall for the final event with the children, boasting their morale and confidence to tackle any situation, and teaching them to balance their emotions during such a difficult and delicate situation is very important. It is actually preparing them for the exam of life, which takes place without any set dates and syllabus but has success and failures. This is the time when we can feel butterflies in the stomach, throats go dry, our voices sound worried, faces turn pale, fingers crossed, avoiding eye contact and preferring to close them for praying in between...Oh God, our heart beats as if we are landing on the moon. Then begins the announcements, with every passing speech of the guests, judges, the anxiety multiplies because everybody is looking forward to the result. We'd wish we could forward this as we'd do on videos, to jump to the prize distribution. Then the declaration of awards commences with recipients of awards marching towards the stage and we'd wait eagerly. Finally, your team is called and you walk along with your students to the dais to receive the prize; the audience is clapping for you and your efforts are paid off. Firstly, you thank God, and then think to yourself, 'Yes! I was confident of this result'. Then comes the photos, press, newspaper coverage which is all common. Then, you inform your authorities about winning the competition, send children back with their parents and return home mentally and physically exhausted but the joy and the moment of victory can never let you feel the tiredness. You'd think the accomplishment will let you sleep well because everything was well done, but guess what? A sleepless night again due to excessive happiness and the thought, 'Oh, we won!'

> *'It is a funny thing about life; if you refuse to accept anything but the best, you very often get it.'*

The Mystery of Taps

'Life is full of challenges', all of us grew up hearing this. Everyone has to listen or experience this and gradually, we'd agree with the phrase. There are challenges right from—fusion of gametes, to our birth, getting admission in a good school, passing year after year to get promoted to the next class, to become well-qualified, get a job that satisfies our head and heart, and fills the stomach with food and happiness.

All of this is not so challenging than the most common and difficult mystery of taps. We visit so many places like restaurants, college canteens, restrooms of malls, and hotels for stay. We all must have seen a variety of taps and some of these taps check your knowledge, technical aptitude, patience, and even the application of your intelligence. All these could be at stake and it may go waste when you try to get some water from stylish taps. The taps are no less than magic; it could be as simple as we always expect it or it may be as difficult as your wildest imagination or thoughts. I always wondered the purpose of designing them each so uniquely; I respect their ability and the creation of this brilliant simple device that releases water, 'the elixir of life', in various places.

Most of us are also hesitant in seeking help just for opening a tap. It sounds very weird that you don't know this; the support staff does it for you, and when you look at him, the way he looks at you leaves you shocked. Something that we feel and assume to be simple, easy, and cakewalk of an experience may suddenly be very difficult and challenging. Most of us, at certain points of time, might have experienced this kind of situation but feel shy to disclose even to our very close pals. I remember once we checked into a hotel in Mumbai, and started unpacking the things after entering the room. My room partner said she is going to the washroom to freshen up. I started watching TV when I suddenly realised that it had been almost an hour now. 'Where is she? What happened?', I thought. I got scared and knocked on the door. She opened it and looked tense, as if she had been struggling for quite some time. I looked at her and said, 'You look the same, what's the matter?' She replied very politely, 'I was carrying out a research'. 'A research? In the washroom!' I exclaimed. She said, 'Come in and help me open this tap so I can get some water to wash my face'. Now, it was my turn to showcase my talent, intellect and use the matter in my skull. The mixed thoughts in my mind made me nervous; would I be able to prove myself or would it be a failure? After trying my best, I accepted that it was not our cup of tea. I called up the reception and got it done immediately. Since then, whenever we go to any new place, the research work begins and it is fixed only when we are able to tap the tap.

This taught me a life lesson that, all that appears to be simple may complicate your work, on the contrary, all that appears complex may be simple if approached in the right manner. In our lives, we too get entangled in a web made by ourselves, then we realise it was much simpler. Somebody has aptly said, 'It is very simple to be happy, but it is very difficult to be simple'. Stay simple, stay happy.

Return Gift

Today, I got a chance to meet the students from last year. I simply went without anything, thinking it was just a substitution period. I thought I would engage them and be back in just thirty minutes. I went to the class with this mental preparation; a few students saw me approaching the class and within no time I was at the door. The whole class stood up and started clapping and shouting out of love and excitement for a while. The twinkling, dreamy eyes of the students became brighter, the smile got broader and their gesture was to welcome and show gratitude to a teacher who had taught them last year. Each and every one was a happy angel and were blessing their teacher for something that can never be expressed in words or any language. In spite of so many well-developed, full-fledged languages, at times, words appear too dwarf and handicap to wrap up feelings and express them the way they should be.

I was so surprised. I acknowledged and reciprocated but I was questioning myself, asking what had I given them that these students were giving me such a warm response? My heart started beating fast, eyes were moist, and my throat choked, filled with love. What an overwhelming response! I couldn't believe it. In an era where we usually talk so much about the lack of sensitivity and emotions, these children and their behaviour contradicted all these and the message was loud and clear. 'Yes! We know what should be done, when, and for whom. We cannot be fooled, our love and concern are for those who have contributed to us, honestly and selflessly'. Immediately, I realised there were classes beside us and that we should maintain the decorum. All of them settled down, I too sat, then another surprise unfolded. Most of them stood up and requested, 'Madam, why don't you teach us? It could be any topic, anything, but please teach us'.

I thought, when most students love to get a substitution period and free time to do a lot of talking and chatting among their peers, these children want me to teach that too during their last period. I instantly thanked god, and felt my responsibility and power. Power, because no one gets such a resource to form, transform, and help them outperform in all walks of life. I thanked my mother who always felt that I would make a very good teacher rather than an outstanding teacher. It is because of this she insisted I did my bachelor's degree in Education. Students are actually the mirror of a teacher's performance; if they love and respect you, you need to always be a giver and honestly treat them like they are angels and are like worshiping god.

Some of them started recollecting memories from last year, whereas, some started appreciating the teaching methodology, some also started discussing about the experiments carried out, others were really surprised that the teacher still remembers the name of each and every student and know them so well. All of these were small gestures but the significance of them is huge for both the teacher and the students too. It was a symbiotic association where both benefited from each other's actions. Some said that I was like their friend and others, their mother. I was more than happy and said, 'I am so ordinary. It is your love and respect, faith and trust that made me feel extraordinary'. If a teacher can motivate and encourage the children then such gestures from the students surely re energises and recharges the teacher with a lot of happiness and satisfaction. No technology, no money, no luxury, nothing can replace this love, respect, warmth, concern, compassion. Strong bonds are to be felt, can't be expressed.

The moment I stood up with a piece of chalk, there was utmost silence and they eagerly awaited knowing, whatever I say is going to be beneficial and good for them. Is that not blind faith? I got motivated and overwhelmed. I began to teach lasting hardly fifteen to twenty minutes but there was such an aura in the classroom; full of positivity and happy learning time and then, the bell rang. I came out of the class after which half of the class followed me; some asked personal questions, some wanted motivation, some just wanted to be close to their respected teacher and what not. I felt as though I was empty-handed, a simple human being but what I got today has really helped me realise that I am so important and powerful hence, I need to be very responsible. I felt blessed and happy. Although I do not have a very huge role in the making of this country, I can certainly be a brick that contributes to building a great infrastructure for the future of our motherland. As rightly said by Chanakya, *'Shikshak kabhi sadharan nahi hota, pralay aur nirman uski god mein palte hain'*.

"Don't wait for extraordinary circumstances to do good; try to use ordinary situations".

Traditional Games and Educational Value

Even today, we cherish the memories of all those outdoor sport activities that we enjoyed throughout our childhood and we actually can feel the famous gazal, '*Ye daulat bhi le lo, ye shohrat bhi le lo, bhale chheen lo mujhse meri jawani, magar mujhko lauta do bachpan ka sawan wo kagaj ki kashti, wo barish ka paani*'.

Our traditional games were of a wide range, from making a paper boat to kites. Something that was common in all of these sports was that they all were cost effective, cheap, easily available, fun to make, remake, and nobody bothered much about sharing. The excitement, togetherness, and team spirit along with the learning outcome was huge. The schedule of playing and outdoor activities were taken very seriously. No fun in the deviation of its routine would be tolerated. Homework can suffer but the sports that were so unplanned, without arena, without wealthy resources were the most valuable possession. Even without any phones, calls, or messages, all of us were connected telepathically and could conveniently convey the time, venue, things to be brought so wonderfully. The connection was so strong that one's tone, order, love, or fight, each feeling was received as it is, without any dilution and change in the intensity.

Gilli danda, *Pittu*, Hide-and-seek, paper boats, kite flying and so many more. The game, Gilli danda, generally played by a group of boys, teaches focus, precision, proper and exact judgement, the correct technique to hit it hard, and using energy when it was needed. Someone hits and others would run to get the gilli back. A whole ecosystem would function in the form of a team, which will interact in a very cordial manner for a healthy sport. The children getting hurt, hiding the pain from elders, and trying to tolerate it quietly was making us tough from within; to adjust, coordinate without grumbling and complaining or even glamorising the pains. Whereas, these days extra protection and pampering of the children has made them very delicate mentally, physically, and even emotionally; a small hurt can result in a big scene.

Pittu, the game played in teams of two, where a ball and some broken pieces of tiles could be considered a luxury. It was about arranging these broken tile pieces as a pile or stack on a raised platform and then breaking it by hitting the ball. In a game like this, again, focus was needed to hit it right and the moment the stack dismantles, the team members gather and rearrange the whole pile. While doing so, they will also protect themselves from the ball that can hit them and be out. How beautifully the prevention of danger while still executing a task in swift and fast movements, coordination between the eyes and legs and keeping up sport spirit was easily induced in the players. Making, breaking, remaking this is what life is about. The enthusiasm, skills, and our attitude helps us to do it over and again on a daily basis even.

Hide and seek, to identify the hidden entity by searching and to find it out before the *denner* is seen by others. Again, a great lesson. To seek and find made anyone feel like James Bond and those who were hiding strategically did so, so that they could come out skilfully without being noticed. Everyone would make noise out of joy but maintain silence when they do not wish to be found out. Playing together, caring, loving, bonding, solving problems, fighting, resolving them, and so much more. It used to be like a full-on 'masala' movie that has emotions, drama, and thrill, adventure, and a huge learning outcome. Wah! How beautifully expressed in the song, 'Aaya hai mujhe phir yaad woh jaalim gujara jamana bachpan ka'.

> *"Have two goals: wisdom – that is knowing and doing right and Common sense, Don't let them slip away".*

School Bag

I was shocked to see a student coming to the school with a trolley bag, which was rolling on its wheels and the handle was pulled by the student in a cool, stylish way. My curiosity brought me closer to him and I asked, 'What is this?' He said, 'This is my schoolbag'. Still, I could not digest it and asked again, 'Do you bring this school bag every day?'. He said smartly, 'Yes, every day'. Then, I tried to cover up my shocking expression to an enquiring and appreciating one and said, 'Wow! So nice…What features do your bag have?' The child got into the shoes of a salesman and like a marketing person he started showing and explaining to me the amazing schoolbag. After so much of it, he said, 'Do you know it has a secret lock also?' I exclaimed, 'OMG!' Now I was totally lost, and was about to faint as the mystery of the schoolbag was revealed. What advance technology could transform also includes a simple school bag, which has a simple purpose of carrying the necessary stationery from home to school and vice-versa.

Like any other person I had a flashback and started thinking of our times when simple things existed with a simple mindset. We too have studied in good schools and a reputed educational board but the school bags were very simple. They were cloth bags, which are the typical sign of reporters, or writers, and may have even been stitched at home; for making them attractive and fancy, extra pockets were made or big buttons were attached. These school bags were, at times, made out of old trousers of the male members at home. We carried them with pride because we knew the value is of the books that we carried and read rather than the bag which is meant just for carrying. Still, we used to carry them with great dignity, never kept them on dusty, dirty floors. We were given the *sanskar* to deal with each stationery item with respect, love, and care. Then came the era of aluminium boxes which were the dream of every school student of that time. They were smart shiny aluminium school boxes and bags, which were handy and liked by all because the corners of the books and notebooks were kept safe and intact. Those carrying them will have an extra attitude, like a corporate person carrying their branded leather briefcase. The body language was very simple, loud yet clear. There used to be a lock and key as an added luxury, if not then a small log of wood served the purpose.

I still remember, a few years ago, when I asked a salesman of a bag shop to show me a school bag for my son. For my surprise the salesman bombarded me with so many questions. He asked 'For whom, a boy or girl?' I replied 'Boy'. Then he asked, 'which standard?' I said 'Eighth'. He didn't stop here; he asked, 'Which board? State, CBSE or ICSE?' This question troubled me a lot. I asked, 'How much difference will this make?' He gave a stern look and said, 'We know better, we sell bags the whole day'. He made it very clear that he will be working in a smart way. I thought 'Oh God how classified! I wish the children should also become classy, the same way'. Another day, I saw my son returning home with a long face. I asked, 'What happened?' He said,

'My teacher scolded me because of the excess weight of the bag.' I immediately recollected our days for getting scolded as we used to carry lesser things in our school bags. Days have really changed. He said his teacher brings a spring balance and surprise checks the weight of the bag, and scolds accordingly. She informed him that if they continued to do so, they may have health issues later. She also said that nobody is bothered about the health of the mind and its thoughts. Now, after seeing the trolley bag, I felt there wouldn't be any issue because the schoolbag is no longer an integral part of our body, it is now separate.

"The art of being wise is the art of knowing what to overlook".

Lunch Box

A lunch box is an indispensable part of everyone's life, especially in the growing years that have unknowingly taught us so many important lessons. If we recollect the olden golden days, when a farmer left for his day long hard-work with some food tied up in a leaf platter and a cloth piece, with *bhakri, jhunka, kanda,* etc. In the present days, there are expensive hot cases available which may keep the food piping hot for long hours. The long process of evolution has changed both the shape of the box and its contents with time. Whenever we talk about food to be packed or wrapped, few questions like—Who needs it? How long should it remain fresh? What are their likings and choices? Can there be a surprise? How can food items be packed so that it's mess-free, attractive, convenient, retains the nutritive value, etc. start tickling the mind.

We all still remember the first day of our school lives, when we along with our excited parents were more interested in what was in the lunch box? In the beginning it is exciting, later, it becomes routine; as we grow, so do our lunch boxes. As the time spent outside home got longer, the number of boxes also increased in proportionate manner. As the young child grows as a teenager, he or she becomes choosy or fussy about their food and the lunch boxes are replaced with cash that is spent in canteens, small restaurants and *nashta* points. Still, in this whole journey from a tiny tot to an adult, there is a complete transformation in our lunch boxes.

If we all just go down the memory lane, we know that some of our friends or colleagues always had a lunch box which used to be the centre of attraction for everyone. Some may not openly agree or show interest but it used to be evident in their eyes and gestures. Some will eagerly wait for that particular lunch box to open, and the mouth will salivate in coordination with their brain that starts imagining what could be inside.

How can we forget the long train journeys and the food in them; they are just the inseparable ones. Even today, most of us prefer to carry home-cooked food and enjoy it, over the easily available food from outside. Longer is the journey, larger is the luggage carrying packed food. Often it used to be an additional bag, which contains a wide variety of snacks, meals, pickles, salt, some fresh vegetables and fruits, curd, and much more. Children will be fed frequently as they are physically busy in the train playing, jumping, moving from one berth to another. All this added spice and colours to the trip made the outcome magical. Sharing food with our co-passengers was another human connection, but if any of them have more or better food than ours, the saliva will choke our throats and eyes will stick to it, the way flies stick to jiggery.

Actually, packing food, planning the *tiffin* is a unique combination of creative science and art because the food should first appear pleasing to the eyes and then the taste buds. I still remember one of my colleagues, as a professional, the way he packed his food in a huge lunch box; starting from green salad, pickle, to sweets and *mukhwaas*. It was like your favourite menu squeezed in a confined box in an eye-catching manner. Even a person who was not feeling hungry would also feel like having a bite from that lunch box. This art is very well-known to all the mothers; it's like delicious food wrapped in the warmth of mother's blessings, love, and care.

Today, unfortunately, this is done by all the restaurants and outlets, packed in so many wonderful ways, carried by many on their bikes in a hurry to drop and deliver the food in the stipulated time. The food is moving, running in all possible directions in the boxes, bags, locals, and cover a very long journey to fulfil endless hunger but it never tastes the same as our school lunch boxes packed by our mothers. Cherish the food you get and consume it happily, give it priority, because we are what we eat. If we don't eat, we may not exist and have so much fun with the wide variety of food, so just eat, and enjoy the wonderful journey called life.

"Do a little more each day than you think you possibly can".

Confession

As a teacher, you can never have a fixed mindset or make a concrete image of a child because the child is learning and every day new things are introduced. They keep changing frequently. It is not that a child doesn't learn enough from their family but when they join their schools, they are introduced to another heterogeneous group, coming from so many backgrounds. One can easily spot those coming from a well-cultured family and those that consider rules and regulations secondary. They may also be pressurized to score very high, beyond their capacity at times. Although, as a teacher, you should never fix a limit for the child because hard work and determination are the keys that can unlock any limitation.

To achieve high and be in the rat race, at times, parents forget to tell what is correct, incorrect or strictly not to be followed. What a child commonly observes is that if he performs well, he will receive a lot of love and gifts but if the child is not able to do, they constraint comments, and negative statements are passed. Sometimes even hurting the self-respect of the child. This is the time when a student does not hesitate to take up a wrong path just for the sake of keeping their parents happy and showing off, which he knows very well is not earned by hard work but by some unfair means. Most of the time, we quickly draw the conclusion about what the child has done but forget to check the background and understand why the child has done all this and what provoked him.

I still remember two very prominent situations as a teacher, it was so difficult to point out the mistake of a child because she was very confident and simply brought her answer sheet to me stating, 'Madam you have not given marks to this answer in my answer sheet'. I was very confident about my correction because I do it so carefully that such a mistake is not possible but I noticed that the answer was written and was correct yet the marks were not given. Such situations are really difficult, when you are dealing with adolescents. I said, 'Let this answer sheet stay with me, I will check it again to see if anything of this sort is left anywhere else too'. I was tense, I turned the pages over and again. Finally, I called that girl to one of the classes that were empty.

I said, 'I am not mistaken, dear child, you will tell me the truth'. I could see tears rolling down. The girl who was so loud in the morning started melting like wax just because I gave her warmth of love and care. I didn't shout. Sometimes bigger problems can be solved by simple gestures. Then she asked if I would tell anyone to which I asked, 'Why would I?' I told her to tell me the truth and she told me everything. She literally poured her heart out and said, 'Mam, it was to score A in the subject, I did this malpractice. I am so sorry'.

Self realisation is the best eye opener for any individual at any age. As a person I always feel whatever comes from within is always far better than the pressure that is exerted by external means. She and I shared a very strong bond of love because now for me she was a 24 carat gold, all her impurities were eliminated to a great extent. From then, we became good friends.

"There are two great days in a person's life – The day we are born and the day we discover why".

Adaptability: A Way of Life

Recently, I watched a movie at the end of which, there was a strong message—Whatever happens in your life, there are two ways to go ahead: One way is to change the happenings as per your wish and convenience, or to accept them as they are and change your outlook towards it instead. The change in you, after accepting a particular condition, is called adaptation. Adaptation to a situation is also what nature teaches us. If we adapt to our natural surroundings, changes, abiotic, and biotic factors, your existence is assured. If you try to change alone, then you might be left out or eliminated eventually.

A series of things keep happening in our day-to-day lives; sometimes it is a man-made situation that surprises or even shocks us. Oftentimes, something that we have never imagined in our wildest thought would knock at the door but whether we fear, fight, or freight is completely our choice. Those who can withstand these ups and downs of life like a ship floating according to the motion of the waves will have hope, for those who give up comes an end.

Some who see a lot of transfers and movements to new, unknown, remote places in their childhood are the ones who learn more in their lives. Every new place is like a new discovery, exploration, and experiential learning that comes informally. The learning and inputs which come in such a unique way are everlasting and interesting. Every new beginning is a welcome door to a new culture, language, food, stories, people, clothing, weather, soil, and so much more. Such regular movements, transfers stretch our skill to adapt to certain places in a very comfortable way as if nothing has happened, or with an I-will-manage attitude. These varied conditions actually condition our mind and body and groom it to become mentally tough to handle any kind of circumstances. This mental toughness is essential to cope up with any kind of situation or problems. Such people find a number of solutions for each problem viz. to solve, postpone, skip, or leave it.

We never find this kind of person grumbling or nagging about anything. They would say, 'Main zindagi ka saath nibhata chala gaya'. These people have learnt a lesson for life which is to *live it or leave it*.

They become extremely adaptive, smart, extrovert, and have a typical liveliness about them; with such people you do not get bored, they are friendly, show interest in learning your language, or may quickly pick up some common words of the local language to become acclimated to this new world; which is a cakewalk for them. On the other hand, those who live in the same place for generations, show a little bit of hesitation in any kind of change, deviation, or adaptability. They may appear rigid at times and it is difficult to change their mindset. Every new idea has to be supported with enough convincing explanations yet you may not know whether they would agree or not. Such people feel that even a slight change would give them a nightmare. Even in simple scenarios, like a change in department or a container in the kitchen being interchanged could also be the reason for an inhouse war. It seems like they never came out of the cocoon called their comfort zone.

The whole problem is because of their rigidity and mental blocks. Not just oneself but everyone should feel comfortable and happy should be the mantra. If all of us move extensively in our childhood, when we are learning, exploring, adapting, and enquiring, then most of the present-day problems will not even exist. All this would lead to a mind that will have an adaptability to nurture a confident, strong mindset which will say, 'come what may, I can handle'. Those who are adaptive are more independent in their thoughts and existence. They learn more and they earn a happier life for everyone.

> *"There is something that is much more scarce, something rarer than ability. It is the ability to recognize ability".*

Goodness: A Religion

I read this somewhere, 'By elevating the lives of others, your life reaches its highest dimensions'. This thought is well demonstrated by the people around us; you may have read about good people on newspapers, E-papers, or watched it on television, or videos on social media. Covid19 has shown the true colours of different people and not their religions. During this unprecedented crisis, we find so many offering help; whatever they can return as a gift to society and humanity. A new religion called 'goodness' is very well-defined by this class of people. Irrespective of their caste, creed, religion, skin colour, gender, or attributes like big, small, healthy, or wealthy, anyone who has felt the pain of others and helped are a ray of hope and positivity. It has proved, to be good or to spread goodness, you actually do not need a lot of money or time. You just need to have a heart that feels and a head that triggers you to just do it. Someone rightly said, 'Good people strengthen themselves ceaselessly', and it multiplies quickly. Holding and touching the hand is prohibited, but touching one's heart with love and humanity can never be a problem by good deeds.

The compassion, care, love, the concerns that move us, the inner-voice that dominates us to do the right and good things for others, the gut feeling to treat other's needs primarily before our own is what's the need of the hour.

Goodness has got nothing to do with what you had or have, how and why not; these questions do not exist when it comes to, 'Service to man is service to God'.

People are helping the needy, going out of their way to provide food, essentials. Some ladies are busy preparing chapatis on a daily basis, others are cooking food on a large scale, transporting it through their own vehicles to far off places to feed those who are suffering badly due to loss of money, work, wages, and so many other reasons. We in India say—'Vasudhaiva Kutumbakam', and we have really set a very good example in front of the whole world. It is not just for the people who live here, but also those who are back from different countries to their motherland that are being taken care of. Government, NGOs, and so many unsung, unknown hands have emerged to fight this unseen enemy that is the Covid19 virus. For all these people, the purpose of life, is a life of purpose.

All religions in the world talk about love, compassion, affection, goodness. Goodness, being the best of all, is rather the base of all religions. So George Bernard Shaw aptly said, *'Life is no "brief candle" for me. It is a sort of splendid torch which I have got hold of for the moment and I want to make it burn as brightly as possible before handing it on to future generations'*.

Similarly, the goodness done to others comes back to you with interest. As Newton's third law of motion states, 'To every action, there is an equal and opposite reaction'. Let us all spread this goodness as much as we can. Let us forget me and mine, and spread love till cloud nine; enough of boundaries and limitations, it's time to be selfless and limitless. Just do well and have the supreme religion called goodness that binds us together to live life better. *Insaan ka Insaan se ho bhaichara, yehi paigam hamara…*

> *"Goodness is the only investment that never fails".*

Happiness vs. Fitness

Mornings are the best time to experience energy and positivity all around you. The rising sun, chirping birds, fluttering butterflies, insects, the light, all other creatures' companionship and the most wonderful amongst all, the humans. We are so alert about our fitness, particularly in the month of June, due to World Yoga day that is on the twenty-first of June. The mantra for this month is *'Yoga se Hoga'*, but the hidden and unanswered questions are—*Kaise hoga? Kya hoga? Kab hoga? Jo hoga who sahi hoga*, etc. The reason I could hear these questions is because I keenly observed the way yoga is practiced in the sports complex near my house.

The science behind yoga is left aside and it is so evident that it became an art integrated activity. The way various yoga asanas are done, it is more of an *'asaan'* instead of an *'Asana'*, meaning it is the easiest way of doing them. I could see so many totally religiously, enthusiastically involved in practicing with utmost zeal without proper scientific approach. It is as if they thought, 'If doing what you like is freedom, liking what you do is happiness'.

The most common thing in all this process is the act of enjoyment and happiness because all of us wish to enjoy what comes with ease; as most of us believe in—*'Ajgar kare na chakri, panchhi karen na kaam, das maluka keh gaye sabke data Ram'*. Few of us still believe in enjoying the fruits of our hard work. Another reason to be happy is, all of these are free of cost—places, pure fresh air, shade from trees, music sung by the birds, golden light from the sun, flash of light of a lightning, the colours from a rainbow, showers of rain to drain the pain, and so much more. All are free. No tax or ticket. We get to enjoy and learn to live with them, to add colours to our lives.

People enjoy exercising to keep themselves fit; some of them want to have more by putting in less effort in less time, such people will have more than one type of exercise. At times, it is difficult to analyse whether it's a simple walk, run, jog, zumba, aerobics, yoga or some innovative technique that has been discovered or invented then and there by these enthusiasts.

Some have it in common with what is the tagline of a famous brand, 'Just do it', some others who were not able to do it perfectly followed the other tagline 'Move on', then there were some, who never wanted to be fit and restrict themselves to the same frame. They preferred to spread so-called *Gyaan* that they gathered from TV, phones, newspapers and so on. They believed in another tagline called 'Connecting people'. Ultimately, the flow of all the forms of energy right from small children who were following '*jee le zara*', to the oldies' '*Jeena issi ka naam hai*', it was a fun-filled environment. Everybody was just happy and seeing them enjoy is such a visual treat; how Corona and other diseases have changed the mindset of the laziest creatures who wished to have the whole world by just a click of a remote and mouse.

In all these lockdown days, nature has shown its upper-hand as usual; it has prepared, repaired itself for a better tomorrow. We all have realised nature's importance and the extent of damage done by us. It has made us that the fitness of our body will be better if the mind residing in it is also fit and fed by positivity; hence, taking up these challenges post lockdown. A positive and healthy mind is an extremely powerful tool that can change the whole system. Now the changes should be for sustainable development; *'tum bhi chalo, hum bhi chalein...chalti rahe zindagi'*.

"If your heart can become pure and simple, like that of a child, I think there probably can be no greater happiness than this".

Grass on the Playground

'Coming together, sharing together, working together, succeeding together' is the mantra that can be well seen at any school playground. It is the most happening place of every school. A place full of energy, participation, team spirit, falling, getting up, winning, losing, injuries, and so are the great lessons and memories. A lot can be learnt here, yes the experiential learning. This is one special place in the heart of every child. It does have many stories, beneath its layers of soil some sweet some bitter, some loud some subtle. I have always seen the classrooms which have the windows facing the playground are the one where all those having window seats is considered a luxury. These are the one who enjoy outdoor activities being in door. They keenly observe all the activities, because for them it is really very difficult to focus on what is going on in the class. Just because they find these activities more interesting, not their fault at all the noise and the games played by the children spread the waves of thrill, adventure, competition and recreation. Some groups play kho-kho, some dodgeball, some football, some basketball and so much more. One can observe a great sense of adjustment and leadership skills popping from some budding politicians, captains, businessmen and even entrepreneurs. These will find solutions to all the problems within their groups without involving and troubling teachers. And yes! They come out with many wonderful suggestions and solutions, even out of box at times. Ultimately the child is the father of man, it is said so rightly.

Such a busy playground hardly has time to breath because it has to accommodate so many classes after class… games period is never a free period. Only when the last child leaves that to the after school practice schedule, it can rest for some time. In this condition there is no possibility of grass growing on such an extensively used playground. This year, after around two and half decades, for the first time I saw a few patches of grass growing on the playground. Although they gave an impression of an oasis in a deserted playground, it shook me very badly. It was an indication of life without liveliness. The students are the soul of any educational institute. All of them are at bay in their homes for protection and safety against covid19. Without the soul of the building, huge infrastructure is simply dead. The classrooms, the corridors, the smart boards, the labs, library, activity rooms dance, table, painting, photography, auditorium and what not has lost its sheen, all these feel corroded with the dust and negativity of this corona disease. The teachers who have coped up well with the change are also not that energetic and bubbly. The screams, cheerful laughter, the vibrations, the love, the smile, the charisma, happiness, the waves and tsunamis of energy are totally missing. As teachers so many times we must have said be quiet, be silent, do not make noise, but the same silence is hurting all of us, we are anxiously waiting for the days to be back to normal and life to normalcy.

These online classes have fulfilled the need to a certain extent, technology has bridge the gap between us virtually, but the social distance has created distance in the way we used to connect, relate, bond and of course the warmth that we used to share. Even if the family is at home all are hooked to their own devices at the name of work from home, online classes and entertainment. We are physically together but have communication gap. The mask has hid our million dollar smile, the simplest curve that can straighten all our works. The mask has also masked our linguistic skills because we hardly express using the best of words, vocabulary and with correct pronunciation and mannerism. The codes used for texting are to save time, as typing full words will need more effort in terms of knowing correct spelling. In this fast paced life all expressions are well compensated by emojis, which have wider variety than the normal expressions. Right from mild to wild, everyone feels if the purpose is solved just by pressing one key, why to type so much and waste time. The irony is the time saved is the time wasted.

Covid19 has checked us all in all fronts, physical distance, emotional cut off, everyone looking at each other with suspicion and insecurity. Loss of academics, because online school education has a lot of limitations small children need love and motivational care. It has financially ruined the businesses and has taken away the jobs of so many people around. The treatment is also very expensive, all in all those who were mentally strong and wise could survive and sustain it otherwise things are really difficult… very difficult.

The grass on the playground also gave a very important lesson, "excess of anything is bad", and the way the human race was speeding and moving is now brought to a crawling stage just by a virus. This gave a chance to all other life forms to grow, because they were the one who suffered badly due to dominance and menace caused by Homo sapiens. The benefit automatically shifted to biodiversity for its revival.

> *"Life's battles don't always go to the stronger or faster hand; they go to the one who always thinks, "I Can"".*

Yes! I Am Lucky

Lucky was just a two and half year old boy, like any other child he too was admitted to nursery class of a very reputed school in the city. His parents felt that the school education plays a very important role in the whole life. So, without thinking much about the fee structure they preferred better formative years and strong foundation for their tiny tot. The extra excited parents started sending their child regularly to the school. Lower classes are the best ones, less to learn and a lot of fun. Actually it is fun filled learning. Be it basic manners, addressing, talking, making friends, accepting, sharing, caring, seeking permissions, wearing uniforms, equality, eating, playing together, saying prayers, holding a pencil etc. and slowly every child of Lucky's age learned all this and their family got an extension. Days, weeks, months, years passed in learning. Class after class, rooms after rooms, floors after floors, teachers too changed subjects multiplied, bag swell and Lucky grew.

Lucky was a unique child; he never liked the traditional learning process which we still have. He could understand everything taught but why to maintain notebooks, Why to appear for exams, and if appeared why we all must get good marks was something he never understood. He was having his own speed and way of writing. He was like all those children who have such questions and doubts in their mind, had speech also, but no voice to raise. To a certain extent he was right also, why everyone should be measured by the same yardstick. All these things were troubling him from within, but he never had courage to say this openly. His teachers also didn't spare him. They will give him different types of punishments. The more he was trying to get along the more innovative ways of punishments and ways to ridicule him were found and executed. He was even deprived of games period; he was insulted and made to sit on the cold floor. He was not allowed to use the washroom even if it was urgent. Lucky was a tolerant and well behaved boy. He being a sikh boy, other so-called good boys who could score good marks would open his long hair and add fuel to the fire.

Day by day the situation became serious and this was like a tug of war between studies, performance and humanity. Ultimately by a lot of hues and cries, finally the parents decided to withdraw him from the so called reputed school. They realised that all that glitters is not gold. Lucky was withdrawn from this CBSE school and was now admitted to a new state board school. He was hesitant because of his background, but……

The new school began like a fresh new page in the diary of Lucky's life. The best and unexpected thing was his classmates, who soon became his friends. These fellow mates didn't compete, abused or teased but they helped, assisted, counselled and supported both mentally and psychologically. Lucky was in a complete transforming mode. All those acts which were pointed to him as you can't, you won't as now you can, you would, and you surely will. This was like a detoxification of thoughts of parents and family too. Teachers were genuinely taking care of Lucky and he who was timid, under confident, poorly scoring person became rather emerged out as super confident, smart, strong, sensible, sensitive human being, yes he is Lakhvinder Singh. All that he experienced became like the harsh rubbing sensation which is a must to shape a gem. The more it bears, the more it shines and reflects.

It is so easy to brand, abuse, label or pass comments and add in making things turn bad to worse, but equally difficult to bring out the positive change. These positive strokes bring out the subtle better side of the person. Such a change always helps individuals like, Lucky to see the brighter side of life. It was the turning point of Lucky's life and guess what! Today Lakhvinder is a Financer in a renowned Multinational Company with a hefty package. He understood the importance of learning with interest and hard work. He could also know the difference between friends and good friends. His dedicated work was paid well by a promotion during the lockdown situation. Lucky is a real life hero, who has survived tough teenage years with great learning without mentally becoming weak and misbehaving……If you have the ability to see the brighter side you will always be a winner like Lucky.

Music Heals ♫♪♫♪

"Making hell out of the heaven or heaven out of hell……It's all up to us". We read about so many unpleasant mishaps in our newspapers on daily basis. We all show a bit of our concern and a thought for the diseased and his family and all our sympathy sublimes with time. Among so many deadly accidents, electrocutions, robbery the most common is the chain snatching.

A team of two bikers on their latest, powerful bikes come closer to their set target and within no time, in a very crisp trained manner the pillion rider will snatch the chain and they will soon disappear, as if they never existed there. These are the ones who wish to make easy and instant money, by attacking the innocent public. A similar incident occurred with a very close neighbour of mine. I then realised for the first time that a chain snatching incident actually evokes a chain of reaction as consequences. That is the time when one realises, how precious our life is, if we are alive we are still the richest.

My neighbour was for her evening walk and on a lonely road, all of a sudden like a flash of light these antisocial elements came from behind and snatched her gold chain by pushing her hard. The impact was so hard that she fell on the ground and her head banged the divider. She became unconscious, people nearby started gathering and soon a group got collected on the spot, to find about her identity, address and rest of the things. That particular day god was very kind enough; that her husband a top brass in coalfields returned early from his work place and just peeped into the matter. Like any other passerby, to see what has happened and who is she. His heart popped out the moment he saw it is his own wife. Immediately she was safely placed in the car and he informed both his daughters in the shortest ever conversation about the mishap. She was then taken to one of the renowned Neuro hospitals of the city, the treatment began instantaneously.

This lady had two daughters, and like any other mother she too used to always be after them, being girls you must do this, that, this way, that way......if you won't do, how will you manage post marriage, what will your would be in laws say...etc...etc. But now everything was quiet very quiet and the daughters began to do all that their mother ever expected them to. Soon they could manage the whole house and the hospital needs in a very proficient and efficient manner. The only grudge they had is now when they were doing everything their mother cannot see. She would be so proud of her daughters the way they managed all the household chores, without fighting but with utmost understanding and care. It is rightly said, "It sometimes seems that intense desire creates not only its own opportunities, but its own talents". In the whole process, these girls felt like asking the god, is it not too harsh to teach the lesson. God was very kind and operation was successful, she started recovering but developed mood swings. She used to become depressed quite often. Her husband and daughters were blessed with melodious voice. Whenever she will be depressed and low the husband would sing her favourite song of the moive "Ranjhna"...Tum tak... And the daughters will join him. She will get carried away with the tune of the song and this will adjust the fine tuning of both her heartbeat and the electromagnetic waves of brain and its signals. She will become very emotional and tears will roll down her cheeks. The staff of the hospital, doctors, and the co-patients will also listen to this exceptional rendition.

Along with all the tablets, capsules, dressings, saline the waves of positivity, motivation and encouragement would induce the love and gratitude for this lease of life. All of a sudden her eyes will begin to twinkle & will become very bright with hope and she will have a broad smile, her mood is now elevated and the healing process begins. It is a kind of divine, eternal, serene feeling that heals all those who used to be there to listen to this music which was pure, genuine actually a prayer. This became a routine in the hospital since everyone was benefitted, she and her co-patients started feeling better, it was like a support system to the medication, simply magical!

Finally a day came, when she became hale and hearty and was discharged from the hospital. Now the mother is happy because whatever she wanted her daughters to do, both of them were doing. One of them is getting married soon. Music does have the power to heal, this is really true. The family and friends do play a very important role to strengthen the bond which is tested during such weak and tough situations. These are the incidents which clearly help us differentiate between the real and fake ones. It is rightly said

> *"Sangeet hai shakti ishwar ki, har swar mei basse hain Ram, raagi jo sunaye raagini, rogi ko mile araam"*

I Clean & ......You...

"There cannot be a right way to do wrong thing", It was my birthday, and like anyone else I too thought of doing something that can give me satisfaction and happiness. I got to know about a group of people in our city, who work voluntarily to clean and beautify any identified corner of the city. I thought what a wonderful initiative. Instead of just writing "My city my pride", these are the ones who are actually adding reasons to be proud of. Another thing is the name of this organisation, although it is "I CLEAN", but it works as a team and does all this selflessly. They not only clean the spot, but they add extra glitter by beautiful Varli paintings. I think this work is god's work because along with cleaning, the dying art form is also popularised, which depicts our cultural heritage and our traditions at all the prominent and hidden places quietly.

I went to the said spot, since it was my very first day I was a bit hesitant. Still was confident about whatever will be assigned as task, will do it whatever bit I can. I saw a heterogeneous group of boys, girls, gents, ladies working enthusiastically. This group was very systematic in their approach and everything was well planned and was executed meticulously. I met Sandeep ji, who introduced me to a few members there; I took some paint and brush and started painting under the able guidance of the senior members. Gradually my hand and brush began to have better and confident strokes. I was surprised to see, in this materialistic and commercial world, there can be a few who think out of box and spend such quality time and energy for enhancing the pride of this Tiger capital of India.

Just as our paintings coming from beginning to finish, we came closer. Our conversations became more deep and serious right from introduction to hobbies and interests etc. Every now and then I was confirming that what I am painting is in sync with others. The way me and my work was accepted was like milk and water. Then all of a sudden my co painter aunty who was in her seventies, sadly said, "You know when we clean and beautify the spots in the city, it's really very painful to see that people residing the nearby areas, instead of taking care and maintaining them, they start throwing rubbish, garbage there. How can they be so insensitive that they do not respect the hard work of others, the sole purpose of all this is lost. That is the time when we all feel very bad, because it is not only the problem of our city, rather the whole country. A small group takes good initiative by contributing positively and a large group is waiting to bring the things back to square one". Each word she said was so true, that I became sad...... very sad. In our country people just play blame game, this should be done, that is not done...but if it is done, we don't even show our gratitude. We find a very few people taking initiative in correcting, rectifying, cleaning, beautifying or contributing anyways they can. Even if they are done by such creative enthusiasts, the complete task loses its sheen the moment we see these irresponsible people spoiling them than to acknowledging their efforts. I feel there must be something done very strictly to make people get the feeling of belonging, sensitivity towards the whole city and then the country. Until we do this, situations cannot be improved. Ultimately it will be, "I CLEAN……& YOU SPOIL".

The Liberty to a Mental Hospital

The title *'Liberty to Mental Hospital'* may seem different and funny, but our cities will transform into Smart cities in a few months and we will come across so many barriers and diversions. On most of the big iron panels that are placed for the safety of the traffic, many interesting slogans are written, '*Aaj ka dukh kal ka sukh*', etc. These really motivate the crowd to move on without grumbling. Most of us have read and experienced going to Koradi Road, a new flyover through Sadar is getting constructed, on most of the panels there, it was written, "from Liberty to mental hospital". These two are famous landmarks of my city Nagpur, Liberty is the name of a very old cinema hall and of course mental hospital is the same as what we know.

I just analysed each of these words and locations and thought beyond. Although these are placed only in prominent places of our city and the starting and at the end of the fly over, I realised that too much liberty may lead to mental problems. As we say 'excess of anything is bad'; so is liberty. In our society that changes so fast, on one hand, all of us want the change, but very few ask themselves if the change is actually good or were we better off with our own traditions and culture? We had our own way of upbringing our future generations, our children. In our traditional age-old, well-proven methods, there were social and emotional bindings and limits for all.

At times, binding fear of certain things is a must and we should learn from our indirect experiences. Without knowing the good or bad, everybody is changing and becoming modern especially, the new generation of parents. These are the ones who felt they had too many bindings and limitations because of which they could not achieve what they would have. This dormant urge has led these parents to be too liberal with their children, wanting to prove that they are better parents than their own. This new style of parenting is to be your child's friend, to be liberal, give them space, and freedom.

These children must enjoy their lives; money is provided more than they need, a vehicle of their own choice, separate rooms, no fixed timetable to get up in the morning or to come home late night, all of them are equipped with the latest gadgets, digitally independent, wear branded clothes and what not. Anything less than this meant they are not good parents.

This is just an example of excessive liberty and resources. A teenaged child doesn't even realise the value of all this and now, since you have started giving them more than their need, to withdraw anything because of anger or scolding or just disagreement will lead to another problem. Initially, the problem is not visible or the symptoms do not appear to be that serious but slowly the magnification of this problem leads to a real mental agony. The child may start blackmailing, demanding, or telling lies, and the atmosphere of the home and family will become tense. This may spoil healthy relationships with family members, they may go into isolation, consulting a Psychiatrist, and into a state that is very common and that we're well aware of these days, depression would be the end result.

Now let us correlate with the title, is this not spreading a very good rather important lesson for life? Excessive liberty may lead to mental illness of different kinds. My humble request to good parents is to give your child everything but first, check if there's a need and if they value what you give them. If they don't need it, we should never give. Do not be so liberal that he considers you as just a provider and a facilitator. Have a perfect balance between needs and freedom, love to live.

"Life……gives you the chance to love, to work, to play, and to look up at the stars".

The Magic of Appreciation

In the movie '*Lage raho Munnabhai*', when the hero slaps his friend, Bapu suggests Munnabhai to say sorry to him; he also says that it is very difficult to say sorry or admit our own mistakes. It is really so as I have found it is very difficult to convince even the very young children to say sorry for their own mistakes, maybe because they are too small to understand the depth and gravity of this big word and deed.

As I grew up, I realised what was more difficult than saying sorry is to appreciate, admire someone wholeheartedly. I have seen people understanding the greatness and goodness of any masterpiece very well but to appreciate it genuinely, honestly, loudly is only expressed by a very few. The reason is simple; it takes the heart of a giraffe to admire because its heart is the largest. 'Why shall I? How can I? May I?', are the doubts left in our minds before we appreciate them but these words of appreciation work better than '*sanjivani buti*' if said from time to time. I have experienced this many times, so must all of you.

When I was with my parents before marriage, I was the poorest cook among all my sisters and still, I learnt whatever I could through simple observations when my mother or sisters cooked. I was hardly given a chance to cook because everyone used to feel it would be better if someone else cooks, so there would be tasty, tempting, and delicious food to enjoy. It did not affect me much; because ultimately, I was served good food to enjoy without doing anything and that was the best feeling. Still, I remember always being treated as a support staff, who would just be following the instructions to get things, keep it back and so on. Since I was not left with any other option, I did all that, and later enjoyed the food. This was a regular occurrence.

When I got married and came to my in-laws place, I was very hesitant to cook because of my background. One day, my mother-in-law asked me to prepare food and my heart sank. I went inside the kitchen and started recollecting all the embarrassing comments passed by my sisters about my poor cooking skills. Still, I plucked up my courage and began preparing. I cooked *koftas*, within an hour, with an utmost horror and with a timid heart, I served it to the family members starting with my father-in-law. Immediately after that, I ran into the kitchen thinking about the feedback and also murmured all the prayers I knew waiting for the result. My mind that was ready for criticism started weaving so many stories on its own. Then, I heard my father-in-law calling me, I went and stood in front of him like a student whose result was to be declared. He handed over a hundred rupees note to me and said, 'Wonderful! This is very tasty food. God bless you. Accept this as a small token of appreciation'. Before I could notice, tears rolled down my cheeks. He asked, 'What happened? Why are you crying?' I simply replied, 'Let my tag of being a poor cook wash away with these tears'. I suddenly felt a great power within me, and eventually, emerged as a good cook. From that day, whenever anyone has tasted the food cooked by me, has always complimented me for good cooking and taste. That was the day I realised the magic of appreciation. He and all the members of my family appreciate it very loudly and clearly. This induces the confidence and courage to be better and better.

Most of the time, it is felt that if you appreciate someone, they might develop a casual demeanour or an attitude but the fact is that appreciation, motivation, encouragement, acknowledgement works like magic. Their effects are life-changing and everlasting. This is irrespective of age, gender, occupation, class, etc. It can be done free of cost and has the tremendous power to transform one from being ordinary to extraordinary, leaving them feeling positive and happy. Wherever or whenever you get a chance, just appreciate, admire, encourage and experience the magic around you. Take time to genuinely appreciate good deeds, and see how they multiply.

"The joy that you give to others is the joy that comes back to you".

The Titanic and Covid19

All of us have been in a lockdown for the first time; it has churned our thought process completely. This has resulted in the change of our attitude towards life and even the things around us. It is very important to stay calm, positive, and healthy physically, mentally, emotionally spiritually, so that these difficult days pass like a bad, sad dream.

The digital connect has really helped us pass our time at home, mainly the television, every channel is re-telecasting the best of their programmes, serials, talk shows, matches, movies, etc. This is a symbiotic situation in which viewers are being benefited as they get to watch their favourite programs and the channel gets good TRP and sponsors. I was watching the movie Titanic, a movie that I must have seen a dozen times or more, but today while watching, I related it with the present-day situation and as I started establishing connections, the whole picture depicted the current crisis so logically and beautifully.

In the beginning, a parallel could be drawn between the people boarding the Royal Titanic to the way our lives were going on smoothly, happily in a much faster pace and how the society was divided into religion, caste, creed, rich, poor, and so on. Then, we see the luxury of the ship, the same way as we, the humans, have exploited and overexploited nature for our own benefits and convenience. The luxury doesn't come free of cost rather at the cost of so many other creatures and entities to whom earth equally belongs. The smooth sailing ship and its other activities, including the melodrama, are the depiction of our routine, day-to-day life situations, challenges, adventures, mood swings, etc.

Now, the invisible Covid19 virus is like the unseen iceberg, which has attacked all of a sudden, changing the whole scene, and bringing everything to a grinding halt. The engines that were put off one by one are like the lockdown in different parts of the world. People are also running around to save their lives or moving to safer places to their home towns and countries. The team of experts who designed Titanic are busy finding the ways and means by which it can be saved, like the scientists who are busy finding a vaccine or any possible treatment for this deadly virus. We also see the police on the ship controlling the crowd and trying to maintain the proper decorum during this tough situation, in the same way, our police department and personnel are doing their duties without being bothered about their own lives. We have also read about those who are unruly and behaved badly with the frontline workers at different places, as do the rich, selfish people shown in the movie. The policeman threw the money offered to him as a bribe depicting that in the present-day situation, paying money cannot save anybody because the virus is infecting without any discrimination. There was a team of men bursting crackers, like those who are giving us hope for a better tomorrow. The musicians playing music nonstop are like the media working day and night to help us all engaged indoors and remain safe. The other crew members who have a key role and are on their toes are the medical, cleanliness, and sanitation departments. These are the ones who know the situation well but are still leaving no stone unturned to control the terrible state. The sinking Titanic is the ego of most developed and strong countries who thought they were the supreme. The efforts and attitude of handling a tough situation by moving people in small crowded rescue boats is like the equivalent of our country that has done a great job in spite of its huge population and limited resources.

At the end, the large number of floating dead bodies are like the loss of so many human lives due to Covid19; still those who follow the norms, precautions, and fight adversities will survive. Ultimately, 'the heart of the ocean' which was dropped in the sea gave a very important lesson that in such difficult times, this materialistic wealth is of no use. What's most important is our life... *Jaan hai to jahan hai.*

"We are weaving the future on the loom of today".

Life Online

Gone are the days when we used to step out of our houses to get commodities required for our survival. Be it groceries, vegetables, milk or milk products, clothing, medicines, or any small vital thing, everything is available online today. You think about something and it is available, or at times, something which you have never imagined, in your wildest thought, can also be there. People of my generation still feel like having a simple chat of our whereabouts with our regular shopkeepers. Communication and relationships are more important, so we may not even mind consuming our petrol to go to these shops. We may meet few of our neighbours, friends, and may get the latest updates about our own surroundings, or may discuss some very serious political issues in a simple way. It is a very easy way to stay connected.

In contradiction, the present generation who feel like they are so busy and earning so much think why should they go out when everything reaches their doorstep effortlessly. This generation just lives in two words: Package and Brand. 'How? Why? Why not?', are not the questions in their minds. They consider themselves smart because everything can be enjoyed from just a click away at home and don't see the need to go out and face all that hustle-bustle, meet, talk, and waste time. They just stay isolated in a lazy, crazy manner stuck to their closest buddy, the gadget. In the name of saving time and energy, they are just busy doing so many things and often lose their way and focus without even realising; so easy to get distracted. It is not their fault too because everything is offered in such a glittery and glamorous way that it's like a Vishvamitra-and-Menaka conflict.

Earlier, all of us were against buying things online but today, during this covid19 crisis and lockdown, we have clearly understood a new perspective of looking at life by once again, committing the same mistake of trying to be smart and overpower nature. The same parents, teachers, and elders who lectured children to stay away and shun these electronic gadgets are now asking them to stick to them for taking their classes, online tutorials, instructions, home assignments, and so much more. Me and many others also know that these young children and adolescents are exposed to these gadgets for so many hours and how safe they are. This generation is already facing so many threats to their health; on top of that, we are worsening it by imposing the burden of these online classes. The bodies of these children are under rapid growth and development, all they need is healthy surroundings, good food, and positive mental outlook to grow well as a balanced human being. On the contrary, these children are spending at least five to six hours on their laptops, computers, mobiles, tabs, etc. with the headphones or earplugs on; these have become inseparable parts of their life. A teacher prepares lessons for one subject, but a child studies five to six subjects.

Let's see this from another angle also; parents of this present school going children are mainly educated, at least graduates, so, can't they teach some life lessons that no book or curriculum can teach? This can be out of their experiences, stories, life experiences, work experiences, vocational, etc. There are so many things that can be taught without these electronic gadgets. The continuous exposure to their tender eyes, ears, body, and brain can be really very harmful; it may cause damage beyond repair. Everybody is showing a lot of concern and talking about education, but education is not restricted to only books, syllabus, and curriculum. It is much beyond. Why are we not worried about the health hazards associated with these online arrangements that can lead the future of this bright generation offline? I fail to understand how good mental and physical well-being isn't more important than an unhealthy body being burdened and stuffed with a lot of information without any knowledge and wisdom. Please help me understand.

"The larger the island of knowledge, the longer the shoreline of wonder".

Shifting Expectations

'Expectation', the simple eleven-letter word can cause havoc, turbulence, fear, tension, stress, and may sometimes even ruin one's whole life. When this is coming as a wakeup call from within it has a very different force that can drive, motivate you, and encourage you to achieve better and better or to reach the set goals. It may slowly get converted into an ambition that like a lighthouse will give you the direction and an urge to reach it. This can be achieved only with proper planning, hard work, and determination. It is said that a call from within is far better than the noise from external entities. There are so many people suffering just because of this expectation, particularly the children, the teenagers, and even youth.

We find people talking so much about the directionless young generation, but are they actually responsible for it? My serious question is for all those who shift the blame and responsibility easily. Not everyone in this world is blessed to have a healthy atmosphere and surroundings to grow and develop from a toddler to an adult with a sound body and mind. There are a few who are born with disabilities or as we call them, specially-abled. In this case, the complete ecosystem of family and relatives get filled with insecurity and negativity. Although science has developed so much, in many cases, it does have limitations. Along with a specially-abled child, if there is a normal younger sibling, then the condition worsens. All the expectations shift and move from elder to the young, tender shoulders, which can't even realise what it is and how to handle them. Right from early childhood, all eyes are on this poor fellow for every little thing and load of these expectations increase day-by-day, year after year. All the while, this child is also struggling to listen to his inner voice that is completely lost in the noise created by his surroundings, including his parents. 'You have to do this.', 'You have to do that', 'Now it is only you who can take care of everything', and the list is never-ending.

Oh my God! My heart really bleeds for everything that this child has to face. Instead of helping him grow strong mentally, physically, socially, the individual grows weak, timid, underconfident and is under the usual height and weight necessary due to excessive burden of these expectations. Where are we going wrong? Who needs the counselling and help? As it is said, 'Parenting is an art, but all parents are not artists'. Do not impose useless, unwanted burden of expectations on the child. Let them have their own personality, opinion, dream, and desire to paint the canvas of their own life. As a parent, give strength to the brushes, colours, shades and stimulate the grey matter, let the imagination go beyond the colours of the sky and then what you get is a complete human being who is sensitive, responsible, and independent and knows what is right and wrong for him and everyone. For me, life is only six words—yes or no, right or wrong, up or down. Let your expectations be just yours, keep them limited to your own self, do not shift them onto others as your expectations are your choice and can't be made somebody else's burden. Let the child have their own voice rather than becoming your echo.

"Attitudes are much more important than aptitudes".

The Unexpressed

Response to stimuli is a common life process that every living organism shows right from its birth; their ways may vary from one another. Some have a very simple and subtle way to do it, and some are very wild and loud. The ways in which we may respond or react varies to a great extent. Let us talk about human beings who are blessed with a complete series of expressions and possess a wide variety of communication tools to convey themselves. To support this, we have the freedom of expression as our fundamental right. Even so, there are things that remain unexpressed within all of us and that is worrisome.

If we club all the means and ways of communication right from smiling to crying, speech to silence, dancing to writing, social media to a simple call, all of these still fall short at times. When these unexpressed emotions increase, spread, and magnify to the stage in which it starts dominating the senses of an individual, such a person suffers a state we call depression. I think when suppression of expression occurs due to various reasons it is called depression. The reason why we are not able to know about this is because these unexpressed feelings and emotions consume a lot of energy within. The people today are very busy; they have eyes that only look but do not see beyond. We try to show off but we lack the sensitivity to understand, realise, and feel the pain of an ailing, disturbed, depressed soul in and around us.

We have developed so many devices and even artificial intelligence; I wish we would be able to induce sensitivity and understanding, or at least something that can raise an alarm about a person's inner state of being—whether it is unstable, disturbed, distressed, and upset or lacks interest. Today a million-dollar question is, how does one get detached from these artificial things and learn to respect real and actual feelings that come genuinely and true to its core?

In this fast-paced life, we are missing the warmth and actual true relationships because we get bored with anything and everything so easily. The reason is that the present-day world is full of options and we always get attracted to other distant things than being happy and satisfied with what we have. We today just believe in showing off and doing everything for status symbols, advertisement, and cheap popularity. We are hardly doing anything for eternal happiness and contentment. We may be talking, enjoying, laughing, and doing our jobs to fulfil our needs yet at times, there are some thoughts, deep inside everyone that may suddenly pop up like unwanted guests. Else they are buried deep in the fear that such feelings may destroy the present happiness. This makes us sad and we keep thinking, 'Do I have a close friend with whom I can share all this?' We never find anyone and this unexpressed feeling, like a termite, eats away our peace of mind by creating a hollow space within every individual.

It's really very important to keep the brain engaged in many positive, creative, and exhaustive activities or else it becomes the devil's workshop. Being busy with creativity results in a flow of good, encouraging, motivating, and happy hormones in the body and this elevates our mood. It is a must, to have long talks with your parents, friends, relatives, and anyone who can induce positivity and help you get an outlet for all that is unexpressed. Why to worry when you have control and the golden chance to improve however you wish? Why to worry about something that is beyond your control? It is really painful to read about so many suicide cases increasing day-by-day. Surprisingly, it is neither the age, nor gender; this could be anyone. As young as seven to eight-year-olds or eighty-year-old male or female, it could be anybody. This also reflects the fact that the more we develop and get technologically advanced, the more we are getting divided and separated. So many chat groups, thousands of friends, followers on social networking sites yet we suffer from loneliness. This vacuum and feeling of being alone affects very badly as its signs and symptoms are invisible but the impact on the individual is terrible. Such a person gradually withdraws from all their attachments and may go deep into a shell that makes their case from bad to worse. Let us open up to have good and strong relations, connections, bonds, and commitments without any greed or need; just selflessly on humanitarian grounds. I always feel, since we have destroyed so many species of organisms for our luxury and greed, it's probably their curse that makes us suffer so badly, even after achieving so much. If this continues, I am afraid the human population will be a great sufferer, so let's express and respect the feelings and expressions of others.

> 'Respect other people's feelings. Even if it doesn't mean anything to you, it could mean everything to them'.

Good Mothers and Habits

I shouted, 'My lord, I object!' 'Objection sustained'. I feel the same whenever I watch TV and in a particular advertisement it says '*Sirf ek maa achhi aadaton ki ahmiyat janti hai*', is it really so? What are the other members of the family doing? I am sure many will agree with me. I have heard a marketing executive saying in a workshop to his trainees, 'Marketing is emotional, it's never logical'. I agree that mother is the first teacher of any child, but there are others who also complete the family. The grandparents, father, siblings, elder or younger, all of them have a very important role to play in inculcating good habits. Good habits and values are the buzzwords these days. Everyone wishes to have the value-based education system.

When a child, as young as two years or two-and-half years is admitted to a play school, don't we think that the teacher who is taking care of the child's physical, mental, social, and emotional needs would take care of inducing good habits? Good and bad is so easy to differentiate that even an infant could do it. Often, a stranger may also advise or suggest how to correct ourselves; so can we say that only mothers are responsible to inculcate good habits? What about the mothers who are very busy in various activities that they might like to do, or those who hardly get time away from doing household chores all day and fulfilling the demands of their family members? What about those mothers who work a job in a different city or a tough job in a remote area? They may prefer to have their loved ones live with their parents or in-laws. What about those mothers who are working so that they can support their families financially? Some mothers these days are involved in tough jobs that to spend quality time with their children is a distant dream for them. What about those unfortunate ones who lost their mothers at the time of their birth or at a tender age?

Can we infer that these children do not have good habits? Does the time a child spends with all others not take care of their good habits? Do the teachers, coaches, and instructors who forget their own children and spend time and energy bringing out the best out of other children not give importance to good habits? How can we all forget the efforts of Shri. Mahavirsingh Phogat, who groomed his daughters to perform and outshine the boys? Can this be done without the importance of good habits? Upbringing of a child is a shared responsibility of the whole family and not just their mother. My objection is for 'sirf ek maa'.

These days we do find that sometimes, a mother spoils their child with extra pampering, or by treating them like a child throughout their life. They do this by fulfilling every demand at the cost of anything and advocating and justifying wrong actions of their own children to protect them unnecessarily. When it comes to feeding, they forget the child's needs and show extra love which is ultimately harmful for the health of that child. With changing times where mothers themselves do not have a model code of conduct; how will this be reflected in the child? Then, the same mother grumbles and says, 'My child doesn't listen to anyone for anything'. In many families, father too plays a very important role in inculcating good habits, performing rituals, following traditions, etc. Let us not restrict and give both, the responsibilities and credit of inculcating good habits only to the mother. Each and every one is responsible for doing so and we must always tell our growing children that anyone can be their source of learning when it comes to good habits and good deeds.

I actually got the shock of my life when I was at a stationery shop with my son who asked for a chart depicting good habits. The shopkeeper said neither does have the chart nor is it needed anymore. I think it's time to contribute, in whatever way we can.

"Good actions give strength to ourselves and inspire good actions in others".

Our Soldiers, Our Pride

Last month I went to Kerala for an official event and while returning, we found out that none of our reserved berths were lower. I was worried and was accompanied by three children. Due to some health issues, I was thinking of how I would manage; with all these things in the mind, we boarded our train. The train was very posh, clean, well-maintained, and the shock vibrations were negligible. All of us were overwhelmed. I felt proud to see my country's services and system evolving and developing.

When you hear of this from others, you agree but when you experience it for yourself, it refreshes and excites you. You accept that the hard earned money of the taxpayers is used judiciously and properly. We could safely board the train and with a pleasant smile, even the children started appreciating the cleanliness, light arrangements, WCs, and the chart that was having the contact number of 'Coach Mitra', and so much more. During this, we really forgot about our actual problem of not having a lower berth. The ticket checker came to check the ticket and when I personally asked for the change, he said, 'I don't have a problem, you can do it mutually'. I made myself comfortable on the side lower berth and had a question in the mind, 'Who will he or she be? Will that unknown entity adjust for this change or request, particularly in the world we are living in? A world where all relationships are losing humanity and everyone thinks that he or she is the best human being. The moment we feel we are the best, the scope of improvement dies there. All these thoughts were playing hide-and-seek within me, and I was enjoying someone's berth for the past three to four hours of the journey. We all were relaxed as no one came to claim it. All of a sudden, a gentleman approached me and asked politely, 'Which is your berth?' I said, 'First you tell me what you're looking for'. I was slightly blunt and rude. He replied softly, 'Actually the berth you have occupied is mine'. My heart sank, oh God, now what? He would surely not be willing to do me any favour, as the way I conversed with him was not proper at all. I narrated my problem, he replied with a pleasant smile immediately stating, 'You please relax and don't bother. I will come only late at night to sleep, as the rest of my friends are in other bogie'. I looked at him with gratitude and asked, 'Are you army personnel?' He asked how I had guessed. I said I belonged to the defence background myself. He then left, and we were relieved.

Beside us was a group of young, talented artists going to Delhi to perform in National School of Drama at a youth festival. All of them looked so different; hardly anyone had a proper haircut or shave. They were truly artists right from appearance to performance. They were equipped with instruments and started singing in Malayalam, particularly folk music. As spectators, we could not understand anything but everybody enjoyed it; no one wanted it to stop, and most even forgot to get hooked to their mobiles, because live entertainment was far better than the virtual world.

Next morning, the soldier came and sat beside the children. We started interacting with him. He was returning to his duty after a vacation he had with his family. His emotions were wrapped in enthusiasm, with all chit-chat we finally reached our destination. To my surprise, when we were about to reach, I was worried about landing safely on the platform with all the luggage again. I looked back and the whole troop was standing there to drop us safely; we didn't have to even touch our luggage yet we arrived very smoothly and we also checked that nothing was left in the train. I said a big thank you, bowed to all of them, and thought that only a soldier can do this for any unknown citizen of the country selflessly, happily, and with a positive smile. What a dedication! We must really be proud of our soldiers. JAI JAWAN!

"Our aim should be service, not success".

Perfection: A Virtue

'Desire creates the power' Once I saw a simple man, who looked like a support staff, busy cleaning the badminton court in one of the famous halls in the city. The hall was empty and I was sitting in an extreme corner because I reached much before time. I was feeling good because I could witness something much more exciting and unique than any match. This was much beyond winning, losing, a fight of expectations and capabilities, or even outstretching one's body, mind, attitude to show who is better. For the first time, this arena has shown me a glimpse beyond my thoughts. The man was tall, lean, wearing a very loose-fitted old T-shirt and had his bottom wear folded at knee's length, carried a mop, broomstick, and a bucket filled with water. He was doing his work with full concentration and zeal. He was not even bothered about who was there and who wasn't, it was just him and his work. He was completely engrossed, lost in his work, and was striving hard to do it better than what he must have done till date. It was so evident from his attitude that he is working for his contentment and satisfaction and for no one else. He was not working to impress others but himself. I think this attitude of a perfectionist is great but a rare virtue. 'He who believes is strong; he who doubts is weak. Strong convictions precede great actions'.

I still remember the great music director, Shri. Naushad Ali, stating about the lyricist of the song—*Pyar kiya toh darna kya*. Shri. Shaqeel Badayuni wrote the lyrics 123 times to get the perfect feel of the situation and standards given to him by Shri. K. Asif. This is another great example of how masterpieces are created. We can also say that, when you desire to work or carry out any activity by putting the best of your efforts, you realise it could be way better; this is the sign of a perfectionist. I remember I read somewhere, when Karl Benz got his dream car Mercedes Benz ready, the reporter asked if he was happy, now that he finally got his distant dream a reality. Karl answered, 'Actually no, now I feel I can improve it ninety-nine percent more than what it is now'. This dissatisfaction and satisfaction of doing the best is a basic trait of a perfectionist.

I remember when a student came to me and apologised. She was very intelligent, good, and sincere with her dreamy eyes. I said, 'You have scored ninety-nine point five out of hundred, why are you sorry?' The eleven-year-old girl gave the answer, 'But madam, I promised you a perfect hundred'. Her gesture spoke volumes about the way she was looking at the things. As rightly said, 'Winners do not do different things, they do the things differently'. A perfectionist is a person who enjoys the given work, feels good about whatever is assigned, big or small. These are the one who put the right proportion of head, hand, and heart. For them, time taken to execute comes secondary, it's the quality that matters the most. This perfection leads to excellence. Gradually, you start getting an edge over others, carve a niche for yourself, and set a benchmark. Then, you will be recognised by your work, the quality of your work will speak for you.

In every organisation, place, group, class, or even within the family, we find a wide variety of people and how they carry out assigned work. In all these groups, at least one person will be found striving alone, to stand apart in terms of quality of work. Whether it's writing, presentation, maintenance, drawings, cooking, cleaning, tabulation of data, or simple household chores. All of us like good, neat, and perfect work or in today's language a branded work but the irony is that only very few seriously take the efforts to convert an ordinary task into an extraordinary one. Today, very few parents are strict about good handwriting, correct spellings, creativity, neatness, etc. They simply accept the way it is done and do not emphasise to practice till they become perfect.

Unfortunately, today people wish to complete the work for the sake of completion and not satisfaction. Moreover, you will find most of them discouraging and humiliating by asking questions that may pinch you deep like—Why do you do such good work? Who appreciates your work? Are you paid extra for this? Are you getting any award? Those who love their work do not listen to all this, because they believe, '*Woh toh hai albela, hazaron mei akela.*'

> *"Excellence" is an outcome of good intentions and the right ways to do a work.*

Washrooms

Yes, a washroom! Most of us would not like to openly talk about this small confined area. I think this is one of the most important cells in every home or a building. All of us need to use it as and when it triggers. This is because that's how nature has designed all the living organisms. In every living being, the metabolic wastes are produced and need to be expelled out of the body from time to time. These wastes are toxic to the body and if they accumulate beyond a certain level, they can ruin one's complete health and life. Nature teaches us to remove and shed whatsoever can hinder our proper growth and development; just like with our peace of mind. If we are not clean internally, our external cleanliness and glitter is just an optical illusion.

Washrooms are not only a place for all this. I have heard one of my friends saying that, in certain communities when anyone wishes to evaluate, judge, and know the whereabouts of any family, they look for the way they maintain their kitchens and washrooms. So, it not only reflects the standards of cleanliness but clearly reflects the health and attitude of the family members. Still, it is a more significant place because in this place, one finds themselves alone. It makes you feel isolated and guarantees no one watching or looking at you. This feeling of not being watched gives a sigh of relief. It is a place where every individual is unmasked and those who may appear to be very strong physically, mentally, morally, and even socially might have shed tears or bitten their lips out of some deep pain and anxiety that may be troubling them. It's the time to express what can't be suppressed. It is the place where one washes their face and some tears and redness of their eyes also gets washed at times.

It is a place where every individual feels safe, confident, secure, and knows that whatever done here will be discreet. I still remember a parent saying that since their daughter scored less marks in a subject for the first time, she went to the washroom and cried there for a long time. Oh! What a relief. At least the bitter feelings got an outlet. Many youngsters and adults must have read love letters or have texted from washrooms. They must have even expressed their feelings in whatever way they want, in this closed and confined area. Isn't it not just a place to expel the waste but also a place where one can express or to do what is not accepted outside, in this artificial world? All the strong feelings, tensions, sufferings, anxiety, love, loneliness, embarrassments, insults, anger and even bodily pains, each and every feeling can be just let out in washrooms. It is good that it is called a washroom, a place where one can flush all the ill feelings and troubles which are otherwise consuming us from within. So simple to let out, to relieve, and ultimately making us light and free.

Teenagers and college students may go to washrooms in groups to bunk a particular class, discuss weird issues and may end up picking up fights as a result of body-shaming or passing comments. Some extra smart ones may keep the cheating materials safely, which will rescue during exams and score good marks in this mark-oriented society. In certain competitive exams, the invigilators would have to follow the candidate till washrooms to assure strict vigil. Some may implant crackers also to disturb the authorities to show their anger and disagreement to a certain issue. I once said to my students who used to go in groups to the washrooms for beautifications in a sarcastic tone, 'Yes! As a biology teacher, I can understand the importance of washrooms as a place for excretion, but all of you enjoy it as a place for recreation'.

This place has seen people with tremendous pain and has kept all the evidence behind the walls; it has secretly buried every individual's unexpressed side which just couldn't come out because of the fear 'Log kya kahenge?' We all wish to use the washrooms that are spic and span but very few people have the manners to use them properly. That's the reason we wish but we do not practice or teach our children to become responsible citizens. Let us all respect and keep this place also as clean, like any other place of the house, to spread positivity. This is because it has really kept a lot of negativity within it and has the capacity to absorb every member's unsaid side for a healthy family.

No wonder the walls, door, mirrors, and every possible place in the public washrooms are filled with the text which is nothing but a type of expression. It is because no one had the courage and freedom to express it openly so, we can say that the place that gives room to the suppressed, or unacceptable feelings is the washroom. These are also called as restrooms in western countries because if all the toxins are expelled and removed from the body and soul, it will surely give an eternal rest and peace.

> *'Jahan soch, wahan sauchalay. Jahan ji rahe nisankoch wo sauchalay'.*

Cheerleaders

'Happiness is not a state to reach at, but a manner of travelling'. The phrase say cheers or say cheese, supported with laughter and noise, is a sign of happiness, excitement, enthusiasm, celebration, and presence of energy. We all work very hard in our own ways to ultimately get this happiness. We have always read in books or heard from great spiritual leaders preaching to create happiness because it is something very unique, in the sense, when you divide it among all your loved ones it multiplies and magnifies.

I was surprised to find people who amplify the magnitude of other's happiness from their heart and soul. It was a wedding ceremony; it was unlike the olden days where the relatives and family members took responsibility for all the arrangement of programmes, dance, etc. Even in many Hindi movies including—*Hum aapke hain kaun* and *Dilwale dulhaniya le jayenge* had such scenes which we enjoy even today. It is rightly said, 'Enthusiasm, a little thing that makes a big difference'.

Things have really changed a lot with changing lifestyles and job profiles. All the freshers think most of the job opportunities are better in metro cities and that the city where they are born and studied until now has got nothing to offer. Their dreams are big; this is acceptable in a few cases but when such guests are invited for the functions, they have a real tight schedule of their stay, will attend the function and leave at the earliest. In such a situation these days, a person called event manager plays a vital role and he will have some creative team members who convert a simple wedding to a very special, unique experience for all those who are attending along with the bride and groom. These people are specialised in making any occasion memorable for the entire family. Their team consists of young enthusiasts who will choreograph the entry, exit, movement to the stage, guest's stay and almost everything. I was really shocked to see the zeal, enthusiasm, expressions, energy, and body language of each of these dancers who were really put in the right proportion to make the ceremony very special. The costumes, the makeup, dance steps, and their moves, everything was properly rehearsed and was in perfect sync. It is really creditable to be able to enact live in front of thousands of people just to make their day memorable, what a lovely contribution. The secret of happiness is not in doing what one likes but in liking what one does.

I was also reminded of all those songs in movies where hundreds of dancers dance behind the hero and heroine to elevate the level of creativity. They are paid so much less, the camera hardly focuses them, we don't ever see their faces properly but collectively they create a magical effect. All these don't affect their inputs in terms of zeal and interest. Even the cheer girls who are ready instantly to dance at the moment a four or six is hit or if some player gets declared out have an awesome energy and enthusiasm and is of immense importance to capture the electrifying moments. Even just by looking at them one can feel happy and energetic, they are rightly called the cheer girls. They cheer the mood of the whole public gathering with their performance. We don't even think about their health or the money that is paid to them. They are creating, enhancing, and amplifying happiness manifold for others. I truly respect the art of playing a role of the catalyst and just being there in the moment. Everyone simply gets carried away by their dance moves and enjoys it. They are also humans; behind all the happiness, smile, and moves there can be hidden pains. Why she chose to become a cheer dancer, is all well? Is all the happiness that she is depicting real or plastic, to mask her struggles inside? But whatever it is, just chill and enjoy.

The way these people wrap their backgrounds and pain under their smiling faces is superb. I respect this human spirit. May these cheerleaders enhance and enlighten every sick, sad person's mood to bless them with few moments of happiness, even if it is a temporary one. The relaxation of facial muscles and the release of happy hormones is just a relieving experience. They are really the ambassador of this bliss called happiness. Cheers!

> *'Always laugh when you can, it is cheap medicine, merriment is a philosophy not well understood. It is the sunny side of existence'.*

Development vs. Deforestation

My city is in a transformation mode, which will soon be a smart city instead of a regular city. In this process, a lot of developmental works are being done in every corner of the city in the last five years or so. In a way it is good to develop, grow, and advance, change, update, upgrade, and to be latest. My question is, but at what cost? Thousands of trees are cut, encroachments removed, soil dug indiscriminately, cement in the air, water used and wasted, use of huge machinery that causes noise, air, soil pollution. It has completely taken over the city. What has happened during these processes is the shift in state government authorities due to which the work that was carried out at the speed of a snail has now completely stopped. So, we are neither a resident of a city nor a smart city. All of us need to be smart enough to take care and reach our destinations safely. There could be a sudden heap of dust, stack of tiles, Jcbs, potholes anywhere, waiting to welcome you. At times, I think if it is really necessary to spend so much on all of this, or if maintaining our resources well would serve the purpose. Installation of so many CCTV cameras in the city, many of which are non-functional too is also a waste of hard-earned money of the honest tax payers. Rather this money could have been used to revive the government schools, developing plantations, hiring people to work on contractual basis to impose a fine on all those who are not following the traffic rules. This will help us generate employment for jobless people. Why are we not using the resources wisely? Why do we feel the need to see our city glittery over green? There is no need for all these things; we must invest the same amount of money in improving the infrastructure of our schools and education. Let us make our schools smart and its students worthy citizens. Let us not just talk about external beauty instead of the internal character. Let us not teach the children and citizens about their fundamental rights till each of them follow their fundamental duties towards the nation.

Whatever be the changes, when it comes from within, the results are magical than when they're externally imposed. The cost of all this developmental work is huge. I have heard politicians pitching them very proudly but do they actually feel this is right? The amount that can be calculated and estimated is spent on all the visible things; what about all the things that we lost which we could not see, but always felt and realised.

Yesterday, I saw a long line of birds sitting on an electric wire. All of them were quiet and sad because none of them were chirping or jumping out of excitement and enthusiasm. I looked here and there to find any reasonable cause. A huge tree, again sacrificed for the so-called development, was laying in pieces on the roadside. This tree was the home to all these birds and it was their time to return to it and roost, but alas! Today they are homeless for the rest of their lives. So many nests, insects, worms, moths, microbes all have lost their homes. I could feel the pain of all these creatures and deeply thought that it's not just a tree but it's a factory that was destroyed, as it was converting carbon dioxide to oxygen in a substantial amount free of cost, day and night without asking for anything in return. It was a habitat of so many visible and invisible creatures living and having a strong bond as we do with our homes. It was transpiring water vapours to help in the water cycle and keep the surroundings cool. It was holding the soil and must have attracted thousands of microorganisms for making the soil fertile in a natural way as a medium of life support. It helps humans to take shelter when it is forty-seven or forty-eight degrees centigrade in the summer or if it rains all of a sudden, it helps hang the banners, to nail the boards on it, and so on. It had its own biodiversity park on its huge body, where all the living organisms were living in perfect harmony, coordination in a symbiotic association. We just see a tree; I wish we had eyes to see beyond. We do not realise the loss in the sheer name of development. Each road widening, constructions of metro, flyovers, power stations, railway stations, etc. are done so on the graves of all these speechless, helpless kind companions of ours. We teach about sustainable development in our school curriculum, how hollow is it? We talk about experiential learning, but the experience is far from learning, in other words, we can say, we do not practice what we preach.

"Today's preparation determines tomorrow's achievement".

Hmm vs Mmm

Sounds play a very important role in our day-to-day lives. It is these sounds which were the means of communication before human civilization. Even a baby first learns to make peculiar sounds to convey and then, learns a language. Even today, when we have so many well-developed, full-fledged languages, so many ways to communicate our feelings with great vocabulary, decorative words, stylish accent, and even emojis, etc. Some sounds still speak much more than the words in any language.

Surprisingly, you travel to any part of the world, these sounds are understood in the same manner and you will get the expected response and reaction depending on how you initiate it. Two such sounds that are very common right from our childhood to the end of our lives are 'Hmm' and 'Mmm'. Both of these words are so frequently used in almost all parts of the world. Often, we find that words fall short conveying what these sounds can. When any tasty, delicious or a surprisingly new food item is put in our mouth, the saliva inside the buccal cavity is ready to welcome the preparation mixing well with it and taste buds on our tongue start dancing out of excitement. Now, the person closes their eyes and enjoys the heavenly feeling followed by the sound 'Hmmm'. At that very moment, this sound expresses feelings beyond words. This is also the best way to appreciate the person who has cooked; this expression is one that no language can ever replace.

The same 'Hmm' can express so many types of responses to different stimuli. It depends on how loud, how long, how soft, how shrilled it was. At times, it might be a sign of acceptance, or exclamation, or even irritation and anger. You can try this on your own and see the magic. You can feel and understand the *Nau Ras*, isn't it magical? One can even get to know the mood in which the person has said it. At times, it may even be used to express pain, or if you don't wish to converse, simply nod your head and say 'Hmm'.

The other sound 'Mmm', usually has a similar effect but it is used in different ways and situations. This sound is common when someone is extra pampered or is angry or stubborn or in a complaining mode. It may also be accompanied with tapping of the foot and loudly saying 'Mmmm'.

This sound would also be produced when you are expected to answer something while munching or eating. Sometimes, we may not be interested and still be forced or asked to respond, then also we may use this magical sound, 'Mmmm'. If you recollect observing people in front of a trial room at the mall; the one who is trying on clothes and the other person who makes suggestions utter a lot of 'Hmmm' and 'Mmmm', without thinking about others. I like these sounds because they can convey the message without creating misunderstandings in instances where you'd select the wrong word. So, let us all enjoy these appropriately and spread love and warmth to avoid misunderstandings. Hmmm I am loving this...Mmmm... All of you try and enjoy it too.

> *"The giving of love is an education in itself".*

Victim and the Culprit

I was headed to do some important work and was driving my car, during the unlock phase one. I stopped at the signal and felt ashamed. The guilt within me started rolling out of my eyes as tears. Just before this I was enjoying myself so much, listening to FM radio in the car with the air conditioner switched on, and wearing my branded sunglasses. Almost all the accessories were branded, I was taking pride in all of these things and thinking endlessly about myself. All of a sudden, the same way brakes are applied to a vehicle at the signal, these airy, fairy thoughts also came to a grinding halt. Something that made me change so drastically was a simple sight usually found at any signal due to red light. This red light flashed in my mind in an actual dangerous way as this colour symbolically depicts caution, alert, and stop.

I saw a couple on their bike with a year-old child firmly placed between both the parents. There was care taken; the mother held the child with both her hands making it very secure. There was a scarf which was wrapped around the neck of this sweet innocent child and a mask. The child was really too young to even understand why this was being worn. He was looking here and there and I happened to share a glance with him. I could read the mind of the child that was full of questions. The glance shattered me from within because the questions were so relevant and painful. It was as if the child was asking 'Why should we wear this mask? Why can't I enjoy my childhood in healthy surroundings? What have you all done that we have to suffer so much? What is my fault? Why am I being penalised?'

The child's innocent looking deep eyes reminded me of the movie '*Do aankhen barah haath*', in which all the deadly criminals were controlled by the expressions of V. Shantaram's eyes, at their rehabilitation centre. The sight was both divine and dangerous. Without a single word, the child conveyed that they are the victims and we are the culprits. It's because of the way we use the best of everything in a greedy manner, selfishly exploiting and overexploiting all the natural resources. In return, we have released poisonous gases, hazardous wastes, deep-dug mines, deforestation, destruction of habitats, killing, hunting, and poaching animals for food, leisure, adventures, and so much more. We only thought about ourselves and our luxuries. We have done this at the cost of millions of other species who lost their existence because of one and only creature, the humans.

We have baseless fights, nuclear attacks, useless greed, missiles testing, biological weapons, drug testing on innocent speechless animals, disturbing the whole balance of this planet while we have the ambition of acquiring other planets too, interfering with every existing thing and system that is natural, at the name of research and development. We never realised that this planet is not our ancestral property; rather it belongs to each and every visible or invisible creature living on it. What we have done is an extreme of all kinds of destruction and distraction. Excess of anything is bad; now, we all are facing an invisible enemy, the Covid19 virus. It is a small microscopic foe that is produced by the destructive minded human species who is still not satisfied by so much imbalance. Now, when our existence has come to a dangerous situation, all of us are crying and shouting, trying to lockdown cities, staying home, staying safe, washing hands, wearing masks, PPE and what not.

If we could have also learnt to live with nature like other animals and creatures, things would have been better. I really feel like our generation and the one before us are actually culprits and the poor, innocent children born are the victims of this greed; which has made all of us blind, deaf, dumb as we could not hear the alarms, warning bells till the system began to crash on its own.

"Lives of great men all remind us we can make our lives sublime, and departing, leaves behind us footprints on the sands of time".

Be like Air

All of us know that all living beings need air for survival yet air is so light, transparent, free-flowing and fair to every living and non-living entity on this planet. This is great and significant because the most needed thing is free for all. It's good that all the basic necessities are available to all of us from nature at free of cost, otherwise so many would have made businesses out of it.

We can learn so many things from air. It is a must for all types of ignition, a must for cooling, for rain, for giving a soothing effect to the perspiring hard workers yet there is no ego or attitude. Be it bosses, parents, or anyone who is a giver or a provider, be like air. Be important, superior, and dominant; still always be very simple and obvious.

Air helps light and heavy things rise, only if you have aerodynamism in your approach. Air can lift a kite, it can also lift huge air buses but the only thing is that they should be moulded, flexible, adaptive, and assimilate according to its ways. It should have the freedom of doing but do so without losing focus.

Air cleans all the debris created by storms in our life; be it your tears rolling on our cheeks or our handkerchiefs which are wet due to a sad phase. It wipes it dry, it flies away the sorrow, and brings a new lease of life. When feeling low, just focus on your breathing and thank the air, since it is trying to lift your mood and will fairly do the same for all. Always remember, the air about which we hardly think helps plants quietly by dispersing their seeds to long remote places. It benefits the soil by giving seeds and preventing its erosion. A plant could have its family in an unknown place and all of us consume them through oxygen, fruits, shade or even the firewood given by these plants sown by the air.

When heated, it moves up like our anger but it condenses too, to apologise, feel sorry and whispers don't worry. The elders can be like air, to give motivation for the dreams of younger ones to be fulfilled. The teachers can be like air by recognising the potential of their pupils who have the spark of talent and brilliance; let this not be latent. All such qualities should be given enough air to illuminate or to convert the spark in them into fire.

As long as everything's good, be good. When anyone takes you for granted or hurts your self-respect, that is the time for you to become like the strong wind that can move, or uproot big old trees, which is like the ego or behaviour of all those who are hurting or troubling you. When you get calm, convey to them saying, 'Don't mess with me. Live and love'. Air also helps us move on; come what may, just move ahead. Try to rise, if you cannot, help and lift others feel the reflection and multiplication of happiness in the rising and achievements of your loved ones. At the end, just let your soul sublime in the air to make your loved ones feel good about you by the warmth that freshens them up by your presence around. Remain together always, as an invisible support of your values, culture, character, and stay light and transparent to make this world clear and bright.

"The best thing to hold onto in life is each other".

One Thread Less

The present-day crisis due to the pandemic, Covid19 has added so many new words and terms to our daily routines. Also, so many practices are now part of our regular activities so as to prevent us from this deadly virus. One of the simplest precautionary measures is to wash our hands at regular intervals with soap and clean them properly or to use sanitizers to keep the virus at bay. Being at home, we prefer to wash hands over the application of sanitizers. Washing of hands not only involves the use of soap, but the most important element, water. Every wash needs water, if a family has four members and every wash requires around two litres of water by one member, then one wash for the entire family is eight litres, and if this is to be done around ten times a day, the collective requirement is around eighty litres for the family, which is eight medium-sized buckets just for washing hands. The problem here is not washing our hands but the way it is done. The moment we go near the tap to wash, the first thing we do is to unwind it to the fullest so that we get maximum water and pressure. This is almost everyone's experience; this causes water to splash more than the cleaning. We can all do this in a better way if we just slow down the speed of water flowing from the tap. This can be simply be achieved by reducing the turns or threads that are designed to plug the water in any common tap. This will surely give desired results, in terms of washing and the wastage of water which is such a serious issue to be taken care of.

This *one thread less* phenomenon saves a lot of water because it is a collective action hence, results also multiply. I read somewhere, 'It is not thunderstorms but rains that grow flowers'. In a similar manner, the wastage of water can be reduced by half if the elders and children of our families are sensitised towards this serious and important issue. All of us have faced severe water scarcity in the past few years and have realised that if someone can save us from this problem, it is no one but ourselves. Instead of waiting for someone to begin this practice, it's better to start early at every home, as charity begins from home. All of us should always use water keeping in mind its need for future generations, not just today and now. This one thread less practice can solve or at least will reduce the problem.

I read about a huge campaign done to reduce deforestation, particularly of the plants needed to make paper. The print industry was suggested to reduce the font size by a point while printing magazines, papers, etc. Since this was followed by many, its result was shocking, as it reduced the cutting of trees by around twenty percent. In other words we could save twenty percent of green coverage on this planet. Through Covid19 crisis, the one thing we've all clearly understood is that we are not needed for nature to flourish but our existence is not possible without the support and dependence on nature. We all talk so much about climate change, the Earth, its nature, environment, sustainable development, and so much more but if we can't take care of these bits, how will we save the gigabytes?

Let us all pledge that while washing our hands, we will use the minimal amount of water required and spread this message across the families, colonies, societies, and the nation. After all, nature does so much for us for free of cost, can't we just show our gratitude and perform our duties to help it execute its own processes, cycles in a better and efficient manner? We may see our ponds, lakes, rivers, and all water bodies filled to the brim, even in summer. Let us unwind the taps one thread less and enjoy more and more. *Hum honge kamyaab.*

> *"We know the value of things when we lose them".*

Traditional Talent Hunt

We all remember and cherish the memories of our childhood much more than any other phase of life. I still remember whenever we went to our grandparent's place or the native village, it used to be the best time for all of us. There was no school, routine, homework, scolding, and our grandparents were there to shield us and scold our parents in return for being so rude to us or may help them know the right parenting. It used to be the actual holidays and a lot of learning beyond the classrooms and books used to take place.

The best part was we, without realizing, learnt the most important lessons of life and these learning got imprinted in our brain forever. One can know about such a type of learning only when this knowledge applied wisely. Something that has always amused me was, if there was a function, household chores, wedding, get-together, small or big, there was festivity, entertainment, love, affection, bond, singing, dancing, cooking, knitting, *rangoli*, embroidery, and so much more was taught without any formal training or schooling, in a very casual way, or rather, the unusual way. Right from our childhood, the encouragement for all these co-curricular activities was much more than the academics. Small incentives, prizes in terms of cash were also given to motivate. The people used to work and sing simultaneously, this reduced their mental fatigue and has always increased the output without realization. Playing *dholak*, *manzeera*, dancing on any song were all of our family members' favourite pastime. This was both relaxing and polishing. Now, when I see people hesitating to sing publicly always reminded me of how ones talent was nurtured effortlessly back in those days. I also feel like it was more of a talent hunt or an attempted to make everybody talented or an activity to help realize your worth or even to teach you how to manage your own emotional needs in different situations.

Multitasking is a word often used now but it was practiced extensively those days. Our grandparents and parents have enjoyed their lives the most and were still the best parents. We never had to go to the counsellor for any problems because it was cured before the symptoms became evident and just simple conservation, talk, love, and affection clarified everything within.

Once, I had been to the village and found how young teenage girls were given a lesson of making the best, perfectly circular, evenly levelled, soft, smooth pooris by rolling them properly. Until and unless they became the way they should be, the dough was kneaded, remoulded 'n' number of times. The girls were also singing traditional songs meant for that occasion. I was shocked to see them doing this over and again without getting irritated at all. Later, I realized the science behind the process was to engage the mind in singing and hands in redoing; the musical notes will not allow the negativity to dominate and the body will thus respond in a positive manner, in a perfect balance, what a lesson!

Similarly, our country songs are an inseparable part of our life. Even while transplanting the paddy crop, grinding flour, drawing water, handpicking the grains and rolling *chapatis*, we have songs to sing and hum. Unfortunately, digital life has really taken away the earthy smell of our traditions and has filled it with artificial essence. I wish the children of the new generation are also taught some lessons the same way where there is practice but the agony and anxiety are at bay. Perfection and excellence should be the motto for all of us; the desire of doing the best gets imbibed in all young minds without them losing their temper or having fear. All learning should be more of a pleasure than pressure. Let's hunt talent, traditionally.

"Do what you can, with what you have, where you are".

Mother Tongue and NEP

'Big lessons of life are learnt from little mistakes'. I just can't forget the sight of a nursery classroom which happened to be on my way to my class. A very peculiar thing that I observed was a fair, smart, well-behaved, well-cultured, tidy tiny tot dressed up neatly always sat next to the lady support staff of that particular class. I simply ignored it thinking it was the case for a day or two but to my surprise, whenever I passed through that corridor I observed that this child was the only one who sits and chats very closely with her. I immediately realised and could feel the invisible strong bond between both of them but this made me curious too. One day, finally I decided to ask the *didi* if that child was facing any problems because it was the very first year of school; problems rectified at this stage are always good in the long and smooth run. As it is said, at this tender age, one can grasp easily and erase the memories swiftly without much harm. 'Good is not good, where better is expected'.

It was past school hours for the nursery classes, and the children left their classrooms; using this as an opportunity, I went to the support staff. She was busy cleaning the classroom and making it ready for the next day. Since the child belonged to one of my family friends, my concern was deep. I called her and wasted no time. I asked the question that was troubling me for weeks, I asked, 'Didi, does the child who always sits beside you have any issues or problems? I'm asking because I find him having a very close and intimate talk with you rather than having friends or interacting with the two class teachers he had'. 'I always view problems as opportunities', didi simply replied, 'You know, this child knows only Marathi, his mother tongue. He is familiar with only those words and sentences. Both his class teachers are non-Maharashtrians (do not know Marathi). They converse with all the students in English only. He heard me talking to other didi in Marathi on the very first day of his school and from that day, wherever his teachers made him sit in the class, he would slowly move his chair close to me and would ask me to translate whatever they were saying innocently'. I was surprised and could easily know where our education system was going wrong.

Why do we feel bad or ashamed about the rich culture and literature of so many great languages, their origins, and evolution that took place in our own country? I heard Sudha Murthy ji humbly accepting how she thinks in Kannada, translates and then replies. In that case, our mind is working like a compiler. It is wasting its precious energy and time. This is because it is simply converting a foreign language to our mother tongue and vice versa. Right from conception, the developing embryo and then foetus can feel and hear the language spoken by the parents and close family members. The developing baby then grew up learning words from sounds and sentences from words and later came the modulation, vocabulary, and all other decorations. The foundation of the building and the blueprint is just getting imbibed, and all of a sudden, a new, strange language is used and these tiny tots are expected to understand and comprehend. The child feels as if he has landed on another planet. In New Education Policy [NEP], learning one's mother tongue is a very important suggestion. The reason is, if we are learning in languages other than our mother tongue, the mind has to first listen, translate, understand it and then, retranslate to respond, which simply means that the language is becoming a barrier to understand the concept whereas, the same, if expressed or communicated in their mother tongue, is understood without any difficulty. There is also no additional burden of translation and hesitation of not being able to comprehend correctly. It would be a cakewalk and make the concept crystal clear without any trouble.

This will surely boost up one's confidence, interest, and love for subjects that caused hindrance earlier. This will keep our young generations of learners happy. As said, 'If you have made up your mind, you can do something you are'. We have so many examples of people who studied in their mother tongue and later, when it came to higher education, they were matured enough to take up the challenges and were mentally prepared for this switch over. A study says that the human brain is capable of learning sixty-five languages but not at a tender age, when command over one language is more important than making the child jack of all trades and master of none.

> 'Do more than exist, Live…
> Do more than look, Observe…
> Do more than hear, Listen…
> Do more than listen, Understand…'

Flying High

It's almost the year end and we can see the joy of New Year creeping in; new hopes, new beginnings, and so much more. With this new chapter, we all wait for a new round of festivals. Right from January, the festival of Makar Sankranti, which is celebrated all over India for so many significant reasons. So many sweet dishes are associated with this in Maharashtra, *Til Gud*, is so famous and we see people saying '*til gud kha, god god bola*'. We also know this festival has special attraction and keen interest in the children community. They just love to fly kites; big, small, colourful, white, paper, plastic any or many, their craze is just maddening.

Few things that are common and quite evident during kite-flying is a group of children that love flying kite one after the other, without bothering each other. Another group is of those children who run fast, focussed and furious as they are chasing the free-flying kites that are detached. Yet another group of children who neither fly, nor run but are busy quietly rolling the whole entangled mass of thread used for flying kites called *Manza*. Ultimately, a specialised team at all ends perform their duties to the best of their abilities.

Day before yesterday, I was just enjoying the heat of the sun, as it is so pleasant in winters on my terrace and I just noticed a boy of around seven or eight years old, engrossed in tying knots to his kite and his enthusiasm was immense; it was so obvious from his body language. He was making all the final preparations and checking to assure everything's okay. He then began to fly his kite, but unfortunately, he wasn't successful in his first attempt. I was silently observing all his activity; the curiosity, anxiety, and all possible reasons and problems were rectified and he tried again but all his efforts went in vain. The kite was not flying; rather it was getting suspended with the string, so was my hope but to my surprise, the child was not disturbed at all. After a while, I came down for my household chores, but he could still be seen from my gallery.

In that entire struggle, I could analyse so many things about him by just looking beyond the act. Flying kites is a simple sport that each child loves to do. All the material needed for it is also not very expensive, most children can afford. One needs to have basic skills and the most important aspect of it is patience. Every time you fail in flying it high you do not give up; you keep trying religiously with focus. You don't leave until your kite takes a leap and starts dancing along with wind and leaves you happy, satisfied, and accomplished. The entangled mass of thread and the kite getting stuck in some obstruction teaches you troubleshooting; your mind and body starts finding immediate solutions to free your kite. The up and down swinging of the kite helps you know that it's not always important to be on top but being there and surviving all the odds is better. The friends who join you and shout 'Wo kaat', are the ones sincerely multiplying your happiness.

Probably that's the reason why the old generations who have played all these sports are very efficient in solving their problems; they do not run away but face the problems to find solutions. The present generation is more static. They play indoor video games where you are given lives and then you can die, but kite flying teaches you to be a warrior, a fighter, and emerge as a winner. The flying of a kite teaches you so many important lessons in life. As long as you fly up high fighting all odds, everything is good but the moment you are disconnected from your dear ones, God knows who will handle you and how you will be handled. So, fly high, never give up.

> *"The day you take complete responsibility for yourself, the day you stop making any excuses, that's the day you start at the top".*

Stray Animals

Whenever you are on the roads, you see and observe so many things. It is not that we simply go through a road, rather our mind starts thinking, analysing, calculating, concluding, even commenting on so many issues which may not be related to us in any way. Suddenly the speed of the moving traffic slows down and on a straight road, the vehicles start to move in a serpentine way, we murmur about the system, civic authorities, and at times use low-level language too. All this is done to console ourselves, no one else is hearing you yet we find ourselves so impatient, important, impulsive, and react accordingly. When you move closer slowly, you find a family of stray animals having sunbath or a get-together exactly at the centre of a busy road during office hours.

Every vehicle reduces their speed and tries to move ahead to whichever side is left on the road and keeps driving. Again, the brain is flooded with innumerable thoughts about the situation. Who is responsible? Whose animals are they? Why are they here? Who allowed them to sit like this? How dangerous can it be? What if they suddenly get up and run? What about the safety of children riding their bicycles? What if these dogs attack? We start worrying about all these aspects. Suddenly, a very vigilant, dedicated, concerned, citizen's soul wakes up within. The best part is, everyone thinks but no one does anything constructive, and the last line is, 'Let it be…What goes my father's?' {a raw thought} And we move on.

Now, let's look at animals that sit in the middle of a busy road at regular intervals. If we take a pause and look at them and their expressions, they are calm, composed with no hurry or worry; their whole family is with them. They can move the world around them by just sitting in the middle of any important road. I thought I must read the minds of these innocent animals. I looked through their eyes and was surprised to see what they think about all the humans around them. They consider us as fools; the questions I saw in the eyes of stray animals about us were so shocking. 'Who are these humans? Why are they running here and there? What are they earning for? Look at the speed! Why do they lack discipline on roads? Mostly, all are moving in haste, hitting, hiding, jumping signals, and driving bigger vehicles when they're under age. What have they gained by this? Why did they disturb the planet so much? Who told them they are the supreme on this planet?'

'In spite of doing so much and having more than their needs, the family members are not together; we don't have anything but our families are with us. We do not read any book and get formal schooling but are disciplined. We do not have intelligence but have heart. The humans have changed everything but couldn't change themselves that's why humans didn't get peace of mind; we do not have anything but can still be peaceful. We do not need free Wi-Fi, gadgets, networks, resources, this and that. No matter what humans think about us, we are happy and peaceful without so many *gurus*, channels, youtube.

Who is the stray? Who is the animal?

Examination

It's almost the last week of January and along with the wind of Makar sankranti, there is another breeze of exams blowing. Many schools, colleges, coaching classes have begun with gearing up sessions of practice in the form of test series, written practices, mock exams, doubt clearing sessions, crash courses and so on. Ultimately, it is a rigorous time schedule for all those appearing for examinations of all kinds. Most of our roads and squares are decked up with huge hoardings of the previous year's heroes, who unknowingly became very famous like Bollywood stars. I also read somewhere 'Complete course revision in one month and score distinction with guarantee'. I don't know which magic wand or *mantra* would do what could not be done the entire year. Will they induce some artificial intelligence? God knows. In a few particular grades and board's preparation classes, children are not given any break as summer vacations. Vacations and breaks are for recharging oneself and rescaling their abilities, polishing, brushing, and realising their potentials after a year's time; it's required to find the better part that is beneath the layers of all that we see and analyse according to people's opinion about us.

For those appearing in board exams, the atmosphere is like a warfront, all tensed about the monster called board exam. The release of the date sheet by the board is like, 'Qayamat ki tareekh'. These dates will decide the rest of your life; it can make or destroy you completely. The elders are muttering the same word, 'Study, study…and study'. Don't do this, don't do that. Everybody from every possible corner has a piece of advice and suggestions. No one is leaving any stone unturned to do their best. *Tantra*, mantra, pooja *paath*, all that also going on parallelly. Uff!

Do we actually need to be so worried that we forget the poor candidate is our own adolescent, and attending exams is just a part of life and not the end of life? Little tension, planning, and execution is a must for good results but too much of it may spoil the things beyond repair at times. Newspapers are full of such incidents where we read about those who could not cope, plan and execute or those who were forced to take a certain course for being much more lucrative than their interest. Scoring very well in exams has become more important than their life. Exams are just to see how much a candidate could register what he has studied the whole year or the aptitude. It must be treated as the beginning of new avenues and not the end of hopes for the parents, family and so on.

Recently I met one of my ex-students who is doing well in a college and what he said left me in a state of shock. The tone was also as if he was complaining, he said 'I studied so much to score well in exams, and now that certificate is only used as age proof'. Another student shared, 'By the time a student qualifies for a particular dream course in a reputed institute, the zeal and lustre are lost. These are the ones who are running for a good package thinking that would help them get a good companion for life who also makes a great package. Then after marrying and settling down, they are still not happy. We haven't taught them to be happy and satisfied; we have made them dissatisfied souls who are earning more but the peace within is lost.

Let us learn to celebrate exams like festivals; children should be taught to appear for these fearlessly, with a very positive, enthusiastic, and energetic attitude and must always be prepared mentally to accept the setbacks and failures gracefully. Exams are just a part of the journey and not the final destination. Happy exam time.

"Proper planning prevents poor performance".

Old is Sold

I was surprised the other day, when in one of our family functions, my adolescent son was asked to sing a song. It was a pleasant surprise for all of us as he picked up his guitar and instantaneously started singing one of the old all-time favourites, 'Ye raatein ye mausam, nadi ka kinara'. A similar kind of shock was experienced by my children when I started singing 'Hamma hamma', along with the radio. My daughter asked surprisingly, 'How do you know this song? It's a new number'. I said, 'It's new for you but we know it's the same old wine sold in a new bottle'. I also told her that the source is the same radio; so many channels and remixes are presented as if they are the creation of the modern generation. The present-day is when originality is lost and in the name of modernity, people are trying to cover all the old things in new packaging and selling it to make money.

This very act is contradictory because on one hand, the new generation is made aware of old songs through remix and on the other hand, there is nothing original. Actually, many others like me fail to understand if it is good or bad. Creativity is creeping in the form of copying, cheating, cutting, pasting, and to make fun of them, so many masterpieces are distorted, changed, modified and adulterated.

The modern generation either lacks creativity or simply doesn't believe in originality. They are not even scared of doing all this to great music or about the lyrics of all the songs; rather they take it as achievement. These want to find easy, fast, quick, and instant things by any means. So many great legendary people have actually spent sleepless nights, hours of practice doing *riyaaz, sadhana*, meditation with a lot of patience and then offered to the society such immortal masterpieces and evergreen entertainment. Be it the music that was so effective, calculated, optimal, healing, and soothing that by default the listener would say 'Wah!' deep from the heart. Talking about the lyricists, each and every word was so apt, correctly placed, beautiful written in a simple language. The expression was maximum in minimum words. How could those people be so great, to be able to think and display their creativity to the masses in a way that everyone felt the songs were describing their deepest feelings? It used to be the expression of masses by the masters yet they were so simple, humble, down-to-earth, and grounded people. All of them were extraordinary in their ordinary appearance. They ruled the hearts of generations for many decades and even today, their music helps stressful generations get some peace of mind, and heal.

Singers were also legends. What they did originally with less resources can never be done by any machine, computer, software or application. I once heard somebody saying 'A computer can do a job of fifty persons, but fifty computers cannot do the job of an extraordinary mind'. That's why, even today, all of us like to hear the original soundtrack and not the distorted remix. Thank you, legends!

"Take time to laugh, it is the music of the soul".

Live Your Life

Recently when I was returning with a very heavy heart after the funeral of a young adult of just twenty or twenty-one years old, I was in a state of tremendous shock. My mind echoed of all the things the person we lost has suffered and about the parents, who left no stone unturned to bless him with good health. The whole family was one; the strength could be felt by the efforts taken. Still, one fine day every effort, every blessing, all the hard work came to an abrupt end, and left a void that could never be filled. On one side there was the satisfaction of doing so much and spending money that was going down the drain; on the other hand, there was grief asking—Why me? Why such a loss? With so many such thoughts, I was driving and was extra careful because I knew my mental condition.

Just on the next square, I saw a group of boys and girls of almost similar age group riding in doubles and triples and was moving their vehicles in a zig-zag manner, shouting any non-sense. All of a sudden, all those who were around them became alert about their skills of driving to protect and save their own lives. Everybody was just looking at them, but no one looked with admiration or took any initiative. The expression said, 'Oh! This is young India. This is the future. This is what they have learnt in school, college, and in their homes'.

I felt very bad as the one who wanted to live a life with grace was taken away, whereas these are the ones who are blessed with a good, healthy life yet they have no value for it. What a contradictory situation! The parents of these youth who are freaking out don't even know what their children are doing outside. If this is the way they ride their vehicles on a busy road, whether they reach home safely or not is a game with life and death.

I was not able to control myself and many others like me were feeling helpless because these days even telling, guiding, correcting this smart, rather, over-smart generation with smart gadgets is like putting your own self-respect on stake. It is true that when we have everything given to us, we do not value it, and those who value it pay heavily for each and every breath. Oh Lord! Please impart and bless such young individuals with knowledge and wisdom, and not just degrees and packages. Let their package include respect for life, for those who gave them life, upbringing, and everything they needed to reach this stage. May some school, college, university design a curriculum for a healthy mindset and a heart that thinks about oneself and mankind. The energy, youth, vigour should be everlasting and their life shouldn't just be wasted in seeking thrill but to live with life skills. Let every young person be sensitised towards wanting more life than years, more smiles than cheers. Love and live your life as it is just not yours. It is for all those who are associated with you. This life is just one; don't lose it just for the sake of fun.

"Everyday is a little life. Live it to its fullest".

Teacher: An Entertainer

This sounds weird but it is true to the core. Let me explain, we all had teachers right from our preschool till we acquired formal education. If we walk down the memory lane, we would remember only a few of those who were different in some sense or thought out-of-box. Whatever they delivered in the form of explanation, concept, laws, phenomenon, theorems, and theories was done in a different manner. The more is the variety, the more spice it adds to it. Not only this, the way they put extra effort was to make it more and more easy, interesting, and effective. We know something that is simple and interesting or is made easy has to be entertaining. We all are unique in different ways but still to tap everyone's interest and bring it to that one common point is the most difficult job done by these super creatures called teachers. With changing times and so much exposure, things have really become difficult but there are still some common traits in all humans and if a teacher is able to touch that right cord, then she can do wonders.

In any educational institute, there are a few teachers who are more popular, respected, liked or adored by the students, their parents. Why so? This is simply because these are the ones who do not keep their lessons monotonous, they keep adding flavours by working very hard on their own skills; they sharpen and explore them. These skills may include, the most important—thorough subject knowledge, voice modulation, body language, being creative, innovative, energetic, and a good learner etc. This can be further enhanced by some singing, mimicry, storytelling, drama, cracking jokes, becoming very serious suddenly, or even melodrama, anger and all Nav rasas; when used in the right proportion, the teaching process becomes entertaining and gives better learning outcomes.

It is really great that a B.Ed. college is a place where all the qualities and subtle talents are completely churned out of every candidate in the name of internal marks. These activities have an everlasting impact and we have the best memories of them; if they are done seriously, sincerely and wholeheartedly. Be it quizzing, dancing, painting, singing, drama, sports, flower arrangements, organising exhibitions, taking lessons, evaluating peers, elections, and so much more is done in just a span of a year. During that time, one does not realise what is happening but the moment you join any school or junior college, all that you have learnt becomes so useful and significant, that at every step one feels like they can handle it. The confidence of being mentally prepared adds strength to all such situations. A teacher has the special ability to scan the mind and body of an individual. This is because child psychology is also one of their major subjects but, just learning for passing the exams is not enough; one needs to apply their knowledge to achieve the best results.

As a teacher, one should be totally unpredictable; what and how you are going to take up the things should always be a surprise. Keeping all the students in your confidence with a proper proportion of love, care, discipline, and strictness is all that is needed. At times, we may be polite yet firm about what we want to convey. Someone who has mastered all these skills will surely be a great teacher. A good teacher must be a very good listener. The class that is one-sided is not very good, because teaching and learning should go hand-in-hand. Learning new things, technical aspects, and latest gadgets can even be done by the students. Be creative, logical, and rational whenever it comes to problem solving. Never ever be biased about anyone in the class. What a teacher can do within the four walls of a class is much more important than taking every small issue to the authorities. By doing so, we may brand a child unknowingly. Be completely participative and involved, have a genuine smile and emotions than a plastic and fake one.

Teaching profession is considered the origin of all other professions but school teachers particularly play so many roles at a time they are—a parent, friend, teacher, an actor, director, singer, dancer, detective, lawyer, judge, technician, counsellor, nurse, and so much more; no less than superhuman. This is because the class is full of a variety of such individuals who are so different; we see just the hardware which is made to wear a uniform but the software and the inner fabric of each of these have a different operating system altogether. Some are up-to-date, some are very old and may even lack flexibility. Some have good storage and some whose hard disk is good but RAM doesn't support it. Ultimately, if we see a teacher who fits into all these roles with ease like water in different vessels, and if she still manages to stay positive then, she is truly an entertainer.

These many roles played by a teacher is good for her in so many ways too. First, the teacher is never bored of doing the same task year after year. They can keep exploring themselves which will help in their development. They become expert in handling situations with a variety of alternatives. There is always newness and freshness. A lot of energy can be drawn from the young, charged lifeforms that always leave you surprised and at times, shocked. So, enjoy and live to the fullest with these tender, innocent, and loving wonders called children.

> *'The secret of joy in work is contained in one word – Excellence. To know how to do something is to enjoy it'.*

A Burden Called Tuition Class

Gone are the days when the weak students, those who needed extra practice and one-to-one explanation were sent for assistance that can help them compete with others or to be in the same league. Now, the common sight is for students from preschool to postgraduate degree rushing to get help from somebody who feels teaching can be done by anyone and in any way. This results in more loss than benefits. There are so many coaching hubs, centres, rented rooms, apartments, corners, and whatnot. A small space with few benches is enough, even in a home, in the hall room and carpet works fine. 'Who? How? What?', are some questions that still remain unanswered in my mind. Who suggested, and decided that this person is well-qualified and a good help for this particular subject? How will the needs be fulfilled? How would the so-called teacher cater to the requirements of this poor child or student? How well would it be done? No one bothers about what if it is not good and proper? What if it gives a negative response?

The parents today are far more educated and well-off but somewhere in their mind, they have a fad that they should live their life, must get privacy, relax and enjoy because they feel payment of fees is just adequate. As if paying extra fees for the tuition class is going to fetch them the desired result, they pay a lot of money for conveyance of auto or van, which not only carries them to school but also to after school tuition centres. When you see backpacks on the shoulders of each small or big student, you think about how these children would enjoy education and learning if they are made a machine that is just running from one input centre to another. No one bothers or has the time to think about what the tiny, innocent souls want and what their wishes are, what about their unique sense of imagination, expression, love, affection. All these exceptional qualities and virtues are simply compressed and squeezed under the expectations which are never-ending and the ruthless world of competition, which is virtually created by all of us, has made the lives of these tiny tots miserable and restless. Their timetable and schedule are so tight that leisure, enjoyment play-way are just the hollow words heard in huge panel discussions, workshops, and seminars. The bitter truth is that the children can perform very well, just believe in them, spend quality time with them, and try to solve their difficulties by themselves rather than shifting it onto some external unknown agency. Have faith in the teachers who are particularly and specifically trained to deal with the needs of all kinds—academic, social, emotional, and so on. These teachers are such great craftsmen who can transform your child or student beyond your imagination.

The sole purpose of imparting education is to give an individual a respectable, independent, happy livelihood but the things are going in a reverse order, the charm of life is crushed. We get so carried away by the advertisements of coaching centres, that we feel they will make anyone a doctor, engineer or an IIT-ian, and whatnot. The moment the results are announced, huge hoardings displaying their results and toppers are put up on every busy corner and square. No one thinks about those who could not make it. They are the ones who are extraordinary in some other field; they also have equal rights to survive. Why such discrimination? Who are they to brand or label a child and discard so many? Please understand that they are equipped with the skills, aptitudes; involve them in discussing their lives. At least this much every parent and teacher should do wholeheartedly. This is the simple way through which we can help our children stay away from the rat race; this will result in a happy, healthy life, and a healthier country.

"A will finds a way".

My Death

'We do not plan to fail, we fail to plan', this is a common phrase I use whenever I converse on the importance of planning. We all live our lives but do not want to talk about and plan our deaths. We feel it is not good to talk about death, in spite of knowing the fact and its reality. All that is living has to die one fine day. God knows. While death is not given much importance and planning, it can be a thought of only by a wild mind like mine.

One day during lockdown, when we all got time from our hustle-bustle life, I was seeing the old albums which were otherwise lying somewhere we didn't know. I saw one of my old photos and immediately told my son that after my death he must get this photo framed and all should pay their last feelings by looking at this image only. Good or bad, that totally depends upon what I have earned in all my life.

I also told him that me being such a talkative, bubbly, full of energy, fun-loving, happy creature, no one should cry or observe two minutes silence because I was never quiet, rather whenever or wherever I appear, that area gets filled with laughter and noise. I wish all those who come to my funeral talk, laugh, imitate me, dance with DJ music, crack jokes, and enjoy. This should be a matter of enjoyment and not sadness amongst all my near and dear ones. If they do so, it will make my departed soul happy and those who will not do all this, warn them, my soul is going to trouble them with all the extra power I will get after my death. It is the feeling of emptiness or absence that makes us sad but if we remember anyone with good intentions and for positive reasons, we never feel their absence. At times, we become so obvious to some of our friends they start taking us for granted and if they lose you suddenly, like in the movie 'Anand', the void or gap created can never be fulfilled. We all are unique in our own ways, that's why we must respect our differences and individualities, being the designer pieces of Almighty. Some say time is money but I contradict this because only the amount of money you have is known to you but the time left in your life is unknown. So, use each and every moment wisely, happily, constructively, and meaningfully. Do all the things you like to do, which may give you eternal happiness, and not the hollow one.

I also told my son to serve very delicious food for all my near and dear ones; they must send me off with a heavy meal and not a heavy heart. When my soul leaves my body, my face should be smiling. It should reflect the completeness, the fulfilment, and contentment I had throughout my life. It will also spread the message that if I have lived happily, I must embrace this fact of death also with the same happy attitude, no grudges, or regrets because I have tried my level best to live it the best and fullest.

I also asked my son to keep a board near my body, that shall have a descriptive thank you message, which will thank everyone for their valuable contribution by—helping me enjoy my life, helping me learn so many things I was able to, for blessing me with all the love, giving a patient hearing to my foolish jokes, helping me grow from raw to a better person day-by-day, inducing the feeling of confidence to achieve more, believing in me, spending their precious time with me during thick and thin and finally, thanking each and every one for making my life worth living and for such a happy journey.

My last wild wishes are—to operate my Facebook, Instagram, and Whatsapp accounts to know about my loved one and bless them on *'Doordarshan'*.

> *"That it will never come again is what makes each day so sweet".*

Printed in Great Britain
by Amazon